English Communication

Authors Michael A. Putlack & Kum-Bae Cho

Michael Putlack studied history and English at Tufts University in Medford, Massachusetts, where he got his B.A. and M.A. He currently lives in Korea and teaches at Dongyang Mirae University in Seoul.

Kum-Bae (Kyle) Cho got his B.A. and M.A. in TESOL (Teaching English as a Second Language) at Hawaii Pacific University in Hawaii. He is currently working on his PhD in English Linguistics at the graduate school at Sogang University. He also teaches English at Dongyang Mirae University and runs the English cafe ⓘ♡ENGLISH (cafe.daum.net/dyckb).

English Communication 1 – *2nd Edition*

Authors: Michael A. Putlack, Cho Kumbae
Publisher: Chung Kyudo
Editors: Chung Soyeon, Lee Dongho
Designers: Yoon Jiyoung, Yoon Hyunju

First Published in November 2013
By Darakwon, Inc.
Darakwon Bldg., 211, Munbal-ro, Paju-si, Gyeonggi-do 10881
Republic of Korea
Tel: 82-2-736-2031 (Ext. 550)
Fax: 82-2-732-2037

Copyright © 2013 Michael A. Putlack, Cho Kumbae

All rights reserved. No part of this publication may be reproduced, stored in a retrieval system, or transmitted in any form or by any means, electronic, mechanical, photocopying or otherwise, without the prior consent of the copyright owner. Refund after purchase is possible only according to the company regulations. Contact the above telephone number for any inquiry. Consumer damages caused by loss, damage etc. can be compensated according to consumer dispute resolution standards announced by the Korea Fair Trade Commission. An incorrectly collated book will be exchanged.

ISBN 978-89-277-0696-0 18740
    978-89-277-0695-3 18740(set)

www.darakwon.co.kr

Components **Main Book**
14 13 12 11 10 9 8   24 25 26 27 28

English Communication

DARAKWON

To the Students

This is the second revised edition of *English Communication 1*. We wrote *English Communication 1* in 2005 to serve as a textbook for our classes at Dongyang Mirae University. We were pleasantly surprised when a number of other schools and academies decided to use this book as well. Over the years, *English Communication 1* became more successful than we had ever imagined it would. In fact, it is still utilized as a textbook at many schools and academies.

However, as the years go by, changes occur. This happens in many ways. Technology changes, culture changes, and even language itself changes. For that reason, we decided to update *English Communication 1* by printing a revised edition.

We have kept the structure of the book the same. Each chapter still has three conversations. There are still a wide variety of speaking, listening, and writing exercises. And we have kept the pronunciation section to focus on sounds that are difficult for many Korean students. But we have also made changes. These changes were done mostly to update the language, to make some parts more entertaining, and to eliminate various minor errors. We believe these changes have made *English Communication 1* not only more interesting but also more relevant to modern culture.

We hope that both students and teachers enjoy using *English Communication 1* and that students will use it to improve their English ability. Hopefully, this book will enable students to improve their English skills quickly as well.

We would like to thank Darakwon for allowing us the opportunity to revise *English Communication 1*. We would like to thank Trevor Mitchell and his students for their comments about this book. They were invaluable when it came to revising it. And, most of all, we would like to thank everyone who has studied with or taught *English Communication 1* and made it such a success.

Michael A. Putlack
Kum-Bae Cho

Contents

To the Students 4
Plan of the Book 6

UNIT 01 It's nice to meet you. 9
UNIT 02 What are you doing now? 19
UNIT 03 Where is it? 29
UNIT 04 What do you usually do after school? 39
UNIT 05 Can you tell me about your family? 49
UNIT 06 What do you like? 59
UNIT 07 What's he like? 69
UNIT 08 What does she look like? 79
UNIT 09 I can do it. 89
UNIT 10 What did you do yesterday? 99
UNIT 11 I had long hair when I was young. 109
UNIT 12 How about going out tonight? 119
UNIT 13 I want to see a movie. 129
UNIT 14 What's the matter? 139
UNIT 15 I will take a trip this summer. 149
UNIT 16 I want to be a businesswoman. 159

Appendix 169

Plan of the Book

		TOPICS	FUNCTIONS
01	It's nice to meet you.	• Introductions • Interests	• Introducing oneself • Asking for and giving personal information
02	What are you doing now?	• Time • Activities	• Reading and telling time • Talking about schedules and current activities
03	Where is it?	• Locations • Directions	• Stating locations • Giving directions
04	What do you usually do after school?	• Days & Dates • Routines	• Practicing months and dates • Discussing daily routines and frequency of activities
05	Can you tell me about your family?	• Families • Jobs & Age	• Talking about family members • Giving information on family members
06	What do you like?	• Hobbies • Free-time activities	• Talking about likes and dislikes
07	What's he like?	• Personality • Characteristics	• Describing people's characteristics • Discussing habits
08	What does she look like?	• Appearance • Clothes	• Talking about people's clothes • Talking about people's looks
09	I can do it.	• Abilities & Skills • Requirements	• Talking about abilities and skills • Discussing requirements and obligations
10	What did you do yesterday?	• Weekend activities • Past actions	• Talking about the past • Discussing past actions
11	I had long hair when I was young.	• Life in the past • Former activities	• Talking about past activities
12	How about going out tonight?	• Dating • Going out	• Making plans • Making suggestions
13	I want to see a movie.	• Future activities • Likes & Dislikes	• Talking about wants and desires
14	What's the matter?	• Problems • Symptoms & Treatments	• Talking about medical problems • Talking about symptoms & Suggesting cures
15	I will take a trip this summer.	• Trips • Future plans	• Preparing for a trip • Making plans for the future
16	I want to be a businesswoman.	• Vacations • Jobs	• Talking about future activities • Describing jobs

GRAMMAR/FORMS	READING/WRITING	LISTENING	PRONUNCIATION
• Present tense • Wh-questions	• Personal information	• Listening for personal information • Listening for greetings	• Speech organs • Introduction to pronunciation
• Present continuous tense	• Time • Actions	• Listening for information on schedules	Consonants [f] vs. [v]
• Prepositions of location • Imperatives	• Reading maps • Directions	• Listening to giving and receiving directions • Listening to identify locations	Consonants [p] vs. [b]
• Present simple tense • Prepositions of time • Adverbs of frequency	• Dates and months • Daily activities	• Listening for times • Listening for activities	Consonants [p] vs. [f]
• Present simple tense statements • Third-person singular expressions	• Family tree • Job descriptions	• Listening for family descriptions • Listening for family information	Consonants [b] vs. [v]
• Plural nouns • Gerunds	• Likes and dislikes • Strong expressions	• Listening for likes and dislikes • Listening for strong expressions	Consonants [θ] vs. [ð]
• Prepositions • Should & need to	• Different personalities • Habits	• Listening for personality types • Listening for good and bad habits	Consonants [s] vs. [th]
• Wh-questions • Present simple tense	• Appearances and clothes • Being too honest	• Listening for personal descriptions • Listening for clothing descriptions	Consonants [s] vs. [z]
• Can & be able to • Have to & must	• Job skills • Other uses of can	• Listening for skills and abilities • Listening for requirements and needs	Consonants [t] vs. [d]
• Past simple tense • Time expressions	• Past activities • Nothing special	• Listening for past actions • Listening for past time expressions	Consonants [g] vs. [k]
• Past simple tense • When • Used to	• Describing the past • Talking to foreigners	• Listening for information on people's lives • Listening for former actions and activities	Consonants [l] vs. [r]
• Let's • Should	• Telephone conversations • Asking people out on dates	• Listening for schedules • Listening for invitations	Consonants [m] vs. [n]
• Want to • Would like to	• Locations and desires • Making plans	• Listening for wants and desires	Consonants [h]
• Present simple tense • Because	• Health problems and diseases • Going to the doctor	• Listening for problems • Listening for symptoms and cures	Consonants [w]
• Future simple tense	• Trip preparations • Time expressions	• Listening for future plans	Consonants [tʃ] vs. [ʃ]
• Modal verbs • Before & after	• Future activities • Saying goodbye	• Listening for future plans and desires	Consonants [dʒ] vs. [tʃ]

UNIT 01 It's nice to meet you.

Vocabulary

- first name 이름
- last name 성
- Please call me ~ 나를 ~라고 불러 주세요
- How do you spell ~? ~의 철자가 어떻게 되죠?
- age 나이
- country 지역, 지방, 나라
- hometown 고향
- major 전공
- blood type 혈액형
- address 주소
- cell phone number 핸드폰 번호
- hobby 취미
- interest 흥미
- be interested in ~에 흥미가 있다
- free time 여가시간
- activity 활동
- enjoy 즐기다
- favorite 아주 좋아하는
- How do you like ~? ~가 어떠세요? / ~가 마음에 드세요?
- greeting 인사, 인사말

Get Ready — Greetings

How do you greet people when you meet them for the first time?

bow

give a business card

smile

shake hands

hug

kiss on the cheek

Conversation 1 — Learning Names
Track 01

Listen carefully. Then, practice the following conversation with your partner.

Sungmin Hello. I'm Sungmin Kim. What's your name?

Julie My name is Julie Smith. It's nice to meet you, Su... I'm sorry. What's your name again?

Sungmin My name is Sungmin Kim. But you can call me Sungmin.

Julie How do you spell your first name?

Sungmin It's S-U-N-G-M-I-N. Nice to meet you, Julie.

Focus

A *Write about yourself.*

Personal Information
- Last Name (Family Name):
- First Name (Given Name):
- Age:
- Blood Type:
- Country:
- Hometown:
- School:
- Major:
- Address:
- Email Address:
- Cell Phone Number:

Look for your major!
- English Literature
- Education
- Political Science
- Accounting
- Marketing
- Philosophy
- Biology
- Physics
- Geography
- Interior Design
- Mechanical Engineering
- Electronic Engineering
- Secretarial Studies
- Digital Management
- History
- Law
- Economics
- Nursing
- Psychology
- Nutrition
- Chemistry
- Architecture
- Graphic Design
- Business Management
- Tourism Management
- Automated Systems
- Internet Information
- Computer Networks

B *Talk to the others in your group.*

1 My name is _____. (name)

2 I'm _____ years old. (age)

3 I'm from _____. (country)

4 I live in _____. (hometown)

5 I am a/an _____. (job)

6 I go to _____. (school)

7 My major is _____. (major)

C   *Match the questions with the answers.*

1   What do you do?   ⓐ   I work for Samsung.
2   Where do you live?   ⓑ   My blood type is A.
3   Where do you work?   ⓒ   There are 4 people in my family.
4   What is your blood type?   ⓓ   I'm from Seoul.
5   What is your email address?   ⓔ   It's bestguy@anymail.com.
6   Where are you from?   ⓕ   I'm a student.
7   How many people are in your family?   ⓖ   I live in Guro-gu.

Listen

Listen again. Then, complete the conversation.

Sungmin   Hello. I'm Sungmin Kim. What's _____?

Julie   My name is Julie Smith. _____ meet you, Su...

   I'm sorry. _____ again?

Sungmin   My name is Sungmin Kim. But you can call me Sungmin.

Julie   How do you _____ your first name?

Sungmin   It's S-U-N-G-M-I-N. _____, Julie.

Your Turn to Speak

Talk to three other students. Ask them questions. Then, write the answers.

What's your name?
What's your major?
Where are you from?
How old are you?

	Student ❶	Student ❷	Student ❸
name			
major			
hometown			
age			

Unit 01   It's nice to meet you.

Conversation 2 Hobbies and Free-Time Activities — Track 02

Listen carefully. Then, practice the following conversation with your partner.

Julie: Can you tell me about yourself?

Sungmin: Sure. I'm a student. I'm majoring in Business Management.

Julie: Wow. What do you do in your free time?

Sungmin: I like to play computer games. How about you?

Julie: My hobby is reading books. I love novels.

Sungmin: That's interesting.

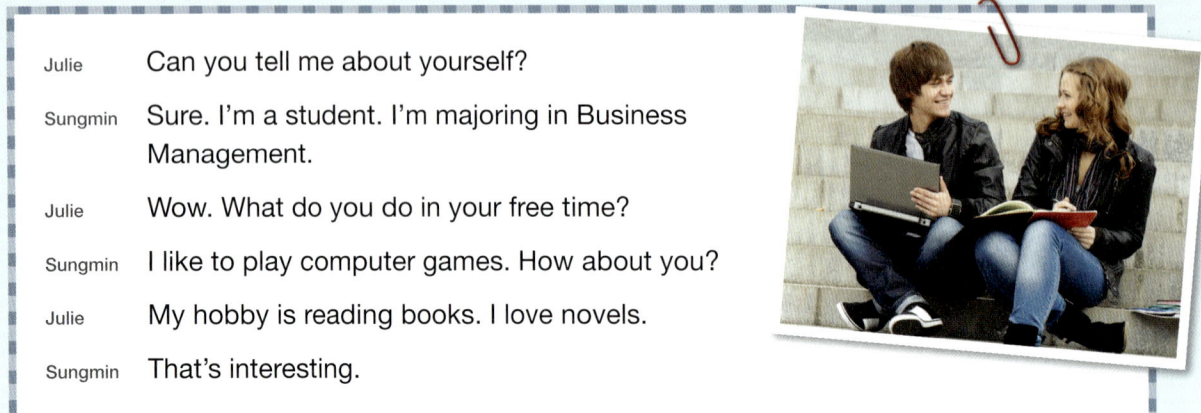

Focus

A *Write about yourself.*

- A hobby is an activity that you do for pleasure or to help you relax.
- A free-time activity is anything that you do when you are not working.
- An interest is something that you like or enjoy.

What is your _____?
- hobby:
- free-time activity:
- interest:

What _____ do you like?
- indoor activity:
- outdoor activity:
- group activity:
- individual activity:

Look for your interests!
- play computer games
- take pictures
- hang out with friends
- surf the Internet
- go inline skating
- go swimming
- go window shopping
- go to a nightclub
- go to an amusement park
- watch movies
- play soccer
- drink alcohol
- travel
- read books
- sleep all day
- chat with friends
- work out at a gym
- listen to music

B Read the list below. Which of the activities do you do in your free time?
Check (✓) the activities. Then, discuss them with your partner.

Enjoy Nature

- ☐ go camping
- ☐ go to a park
- ☐ go mountain climbing
- ☐ go fishing
- ☐ relax at the beach
- ☐ go bird-watching
- ☐ go hiking
- ☐ go scuba diving
- ☐ get some fresh air

Take a Trip

- ☐ visit a foreign country
- ☐ visit your relatives
- ☐ go on a cruise
- ☐ travel around the country
- ☐ take a tour
- ☐ stay at a temple
- ☐ visit a historical site
- ☐ attend a festival
- ☐ go on a family trip

Stay Home

- ☐ watch TV or videos
- ☐ listen to music
- ☐ play computer games
- ☐ read books or magazines
- ☐ play with your pet
- ☐ play a musical instrument
- ☐ update your homepage
- ☐ watch sports
- ☐ cook

Go Out

- ☐ go to an amusement park
- ☐ go dancing
- ☐ have fun with your friends
- ☐ visit a museum
- ☐ go to a concert
- ☐ go out for dinner
- ☐ go to a party
- ☐ go to the movies
- ☐ go shopping

Play Sports & Exercise

- ☐ jog
- ☐ ride a bicycle
- ☐ throw a ball
- ☐ go swimming
- ☐ take a long walk
- ☐ play soccer
- ☐ go to a sporting event
- ☐ go to a gym
- ☐ do aerobics

C *Fill in the blanks. Then, introduce yourself to your group.*

1. What's your hobby? My hobby is _____.
2. What's your free-time activity? I _____ in my free time.
3. What free-time activity do you do alone? I _____ alone.
4. What free-time activity do you do with others? I _____ with others.
5. What are you interested in? I'm interested in _____.
6. What's your favorite indoor activity? My favorite indoor activity is _____.
7. What's your favorite group activity? My favorite group activity is _____.

Listen

Listen again. Then, complete the conversation.

Julie	Can you tell me about yourself?
Sungmin	Sure. I'm a _____. I'm majoring in _____.
Julie	Wow. What do you do in _____?
Sungmin	I like to play _____. How about you?
Julie	My hobby is _____. I love novels.
Sungmin	That's interesting.

Your Turn to Speak

Talk to three other students. Ask them questions. Then, write the answers.

A What's your <u>hobby</u>?
B My hobby is taking pictures.

	Student ❶	Student ❷	Student ❸
hobby			
free-time activity			
interest			

Conversation 3 Favorites
Track 03

Listen carefully. Then, practice the following conversation with your partner.

Sungmin How do you like living in Korea?
Julie It's great. I really like Korean food.
Sungmin What's your favorite food?
Julie My favorite Korean food is bulgogi.
Sungmin Yum. My favorite American food is pizza.

Focus

A *Write about yourself.*

What's your favorite _____?
- food:
- class:
- movie:
- book:
- sport:
- TV program:
- kind of music:
- computer game:
- social media site:
- online shopping mall:

B *Fill in the blanks. Then, talk about your favorites with your partner.*

1 My favorite food is _____.
2 My favorite movie is _____.
3 My favorite book is _____.
4 _____ is my favorite sport.
5 _____ is my favorite TV program.
6 _____ is my favorite computer game.

C Complete the conversation. Use the words in the box.

love	enjoy	how	favorite	best

Sumi What's your (1) _____ food?

Rick Hmm. That's difficult. I think that I (2) _____ all foods.

Sumi Well, choose just one. (3) _____ do you like Korean food?

Rick It's great, but it's not my favorite.

Sumi So what food do you like the (4) _____ then?

Rick That's easy. I (5) _____ Italian food the most. It's my favorite.

Listen

Listen again. Then, complete the conversation.

Sungmin _____ living in Korea?

Julie It's great. I really like Korean food.

Sungmin What's your _____?

Julie _____ is bulgogi.

Sungmin Yum. My favorite American food is pizza.

Your Turn to Speak

Talk to three other students. Ask them questions. Then, write the answers.

A What's your favorite class?
B My favorite class is English.

	Student ❶	Student ❷	Student ❸
class			
kind of music			
movie			

English Communication 1

Let's Practice Pronunciation

This is a map of your head. It shows the different positions and places in your mouth.

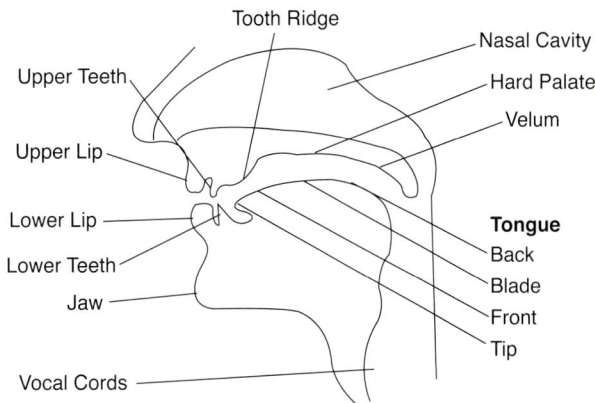

발음기호표

단모음										장모음
[i]	[e]	[a]	[ə]	[æ]	[ɚ]	[u]	[ɔ]	[o]	[ɛ]	단모음을 길게 발음한다.
이	에	아	어	애	어	우	오	오	에	[iː]

이중모음									반모음	
[ei]	[ou]	[ai]	[oi]	[au]	[ɛər]	[iər]	[oər]	[uər]	[w]	[j]
에이	오우	아이	오이	아우	에어	이어	오우	우어	오, 우	이

자음										
[p]	[b]	[k]	[g]	[m]	[n]	[ŋ]	[h]	[t]	[d]	[f]
ㅍ	ㅂ	ㅋ	ㄱ	ㅁ	ㄴ	ㅇ	ㅎ	ㅌ	ㄷ	ㅍ
[v]	[ð]	[θ]	[s]	[z]	[ʃ]	[dʒ]	[tʃ]	[ʒ]	[r]	[l]
ㅂ	ㄷ	ㅅ	ㅅ	ㅈ	쉬	쥐	ㅊ	ㅈ	ㄹ	ㄹ

Sentence Patterns

1 What's your _____ again?   당신의 _____ 이(가) 뭐라고 했죠?
   name | job | cell phone number   이름 | 직업 | 핸드폰 번호

2 My hobby is _____.   내 취미는 _____ 예요.
   hiking | playing video games | surfing the Internet   등산 | 비디오 게임 | 인터넷 검색

3 What's your favorite _____?   가장 좋아하는 _____ 은(는) 무엇입니까?
   food | kind of music | movie   음식 | 음악 종류 | 영화

Let's Read

Questions to Avoid
Asking Personal Questions

Korean culture and American culture are sometimes similar, but they can often be very different. In Korea, people often ask very personal questions even if they are meeting a person for the first time. However, in the United States, if you don't know a person well, you should avoid asking personal questions. For example, in Korea, when people meet someone for the first time, they often ask, "How old are you?" This is a perfectly good question in Korea. However, in American culture, "How old are you?" is a rude question, especially if you are meeting a person for the first time.

Here are some other questions that you should NOT ask Americans and other Westerners:

Are you married?
Why aren't you married?
How much money do you make?
What's your religion?

Basically, try not to ask too many personal questions. They can make some people uncomfortable. As Americans become better friends with people, they feel more comfortable talking about their private lives.

So, if you meet an American for the first time, don't ask too many personal questions. Even though we are in Korea, we should remember that American culture is different, and the person might not be used to Korean culture yet.

Let's Talk More

1. What are some good questions to ask foreigners?
2. Have you ever met a foreigner? What did you talk about?
3. When people ask you personal questions, how do you answer them?

UNIT 02 What are you doing now?

Vocabulary

- busy 바쁜
- have no time 시간이 없다
- Can you ~? ~할 수 있어요?
- What time is it now? 지금 몇 시죠?
- library 도서관
- have a test 시험이 있다
- take a test 시험을 보다
- You look ~ 너~해 보인다
- I can't wait! (너무 기대돼서) 기다릴 수 없어!
- That sounds like fun. 그거 재미있겠네요.
- What are you doing tonight? 오늘 밤 뭐 할 거예요?
- Nothing special. 특별한 건 없어요.
- spend money 돈을 쓰다
- talk on the phone 전화로 이야기하다

Get Ready The Present Continuous Tense

Use the present continuous tense to talk about an action someone is doing right now.

❶
They _are watching_ television. (watch)

❷
She _____ on her cell phone. (talk)

❸
They _____ their homework. (do)

❹
She _____ her boyfriend. (meet)

❺
They _____ dinner. (have)

❻
We _____ a test. (take)

Conversation 1 — Current Activities

Track 04

Listen carefully. Then, practice the following conversation with your partner.

Rick	Good morning, Sumi. Are you busy?
Sumi	Yes, I am. I have no time today.
Rick	Really? What are you doing now?
Sumi	I'm studying math right now.
Rick	Oh. Then can you meet me tonight at 6:30?
Sumi	Sorry. I'm having dinner with my friends tonight.

Focus

A Look at the pictures. What are the people doing?

study	~~drive~~	swim	watch a movie	play the flute
cook	play	basketball	ride a bicycle	jog

1. He's **driving**.
2. They're _____.
3. They're _____.
4. They're _____.
5. They're _____.
6. They're _____.

20 English Communication 1

She's _____.   She's _____.   She's _____.

B Circle the mistakes. Then, write the correct sentences.

1 I am (go) to the park now.   I am going to the park now.
2 We exercising at the gym.   _____
3 My sister is study for her English test. _____
4 They are play computer games now.   _____
5 He is talking to his girlfriend yesterday. _____
6 Mr. Park and Mr. Lee is having a meeting. _____
7 John is do meeting a client now.   _____
8 What are they eating now right?   _____

C Practice the different ways to tell time.

| What time is it now? → It's _____. |

12:00
noon
twelve P.M.
midnight
twelve A.M.

3:15 P.M.
three fifteen
(in the afternoon)
a quarter after three
a quarter past three

5:30 P.M.
five thirty
(in the evening)
half past five

7:45 A.M.
seven forty-five
(in the morning)
a quarter to eight

D Look at the clocks. Then, write the correct times.

1

It's four thirty.
It's half past four.

2

3

4

5

6

Listen

Listen again. Then, complete the conversation.

Rick Good morning, Sumi. _____?
Sumi Yes, I am. I _____ today.
Rick Really? _____ now?
Sumi I'm studying _____ right now.
Rick Oh. Then can you meet me tonight at 6:30?
Sumi Sorry. _____ with my friends tonight.

Conversation 2   Present Actions   Track 05

Listen carefully. Then, practice the following conversation with your partner.

Rick	Do you know where John is?
Sumi	Yeah. He's at the library.
Rick	The library! What is he doing there?
Sumi	He's studying economics. He has a big test tomorrow.
Rick	Oh. Is he studying with Sungmin?
Sumi	No, Sungmin is with Julie. They're watching a movie together.

Focus

A Talk to your partner. Make sentences using the words below.

> A What is <u>Mina</u> doing right now?
> B Mina is <u>reading a book</u>.

1 Mina / read a book
2 Hansu / brush his teeth
3 Minji / do the laundry
4 Hongchul / read the newspaper
5 Eunju and Minho / play cards
6 you / download an app

B Think about your daily schedule. Then, complete the sentences.

1 It's 9:00 A.M. I am _____ now.
2 It's _____. I am having lunch now.
3 It's 1:30 P.M. I am _____ now.
4 It's _____. I am going to school now.
5 It's 8:00 P.M. I am _____ now.
6 It's _____. I am going to bed now.

Unit 02 What are you doing now?

C Look at the pictures. What are the people doing? What time are they doing the activities?

1
12:00

2
3:25

3
4:30

4
6:50

5
8:10

6
10:30

Listen

Listen again. Then, complete the conversation.

Rick Do you know where John is?

Sumi Yeah. He's at the library.

Rick The library! _____ there?

Sumi _____ economics. He has a big test tomorrow.

Rick Oh. _____ with Sungmin?

Sumi No, Sungmin is with Julie. _____ together.

Your Turn to Speak

Talk to three other students. Ask them questions. Then, write the answers.

A It's <u>8:00 A.M.</u> What are you doing now?
B I am eating breakfast now.

	Student ❶	Student ❷	Student ❸
10:00 A.M			
3:00 P.M.			
5:00 P.M.			

Conversation 3 Future Actions — Track 06

Listen carefully. Then, practice the following conversation with your partner.

Jihye	You look really happy today.
John	I'm going to a concert tonight. I can't wait.
Jihye	That sounds like fun. I wish I could go.
John	What are you doing tonight?
Jihye	Nothing special. But my friend and I are going shopping tomorrow.
John	Don't spend too much money.

Focus

A Answer the following questions.

1 What are you doing tomorrow? ___I'm meeting my friend tomorrow.___
2 What are you doing after class? _____
3 What are you having for dinner? _____
4 What are you doing this weekend? _____
5 Where are you going next week? _____
6 When are you taking a trip? _____

B Complete the sentences. Use the correct verb forms.

1 My friends and I ___are having dinner together___ tomorrow.
   (have dinner together)

2 I _____ this evening.
   (play computer games)

3 I _____ tomorrow morning.
   (go to my office)

4 My boyfriend _____ this weekend.
   (meet me)

5 He _____ tonight.
   (call me)

Unit 02 What are you doing now?

Listen

Listen again. Then, complete the conversation.

Jihye　　You look really happy today.

John　　I'm _____ tonight. I can't wait.

Jihye　　That sounds like fun. I wish I could go.

John　　_____ tonight?

Jihye　　Nothing special. But my friend and I are _____ tomorrow.

John　　Don't spend too much money.

Your Turn to Speak

Talk to three other students. Ask them questions. Then, write the answers.

A What are you doing tonight?
B I'm doing my homework.

	Student ❶	Student ❷	Student ❸
tonight			
tomorrow			
this weekend			
next week			

Let's Practice Pronunciation

Track 07

Pronunciation

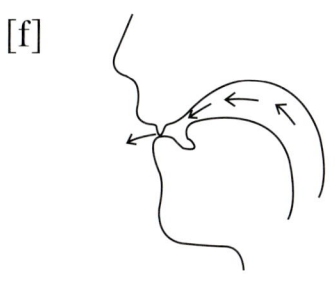 [f]

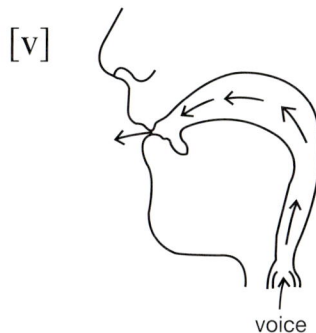 [v]
voice

Word Comparison

[f] and [v] have different sounds. Try pronouncing the words below.

[f]	fine	fat	fan	leaf	half	belief	thief	safe	proof
[v]	vine	vat	van	leave	halve	believe	thieve	save	prove

Sentences

Read the following sentences. Try to pronounce [f] and [v] correctly.

1 It's a **safe investment**.
2 They **found** a **beautiful view**.
3 **Four foolish vampires starved** on the **roof**.
4 The **flowers** in the **vase** looked **fabulous** in **Frank's living** room.
5 She **invested** her money in the **safest funds** she could **find**.

Sentence Patterns

1 Are you _____?
   busy | hungry | sick

   당신은 _____ 합니까?
   바쁜 | 배고픈 | 아픈

2 They're _____ together.
   watching a movie
   exercising
   traveling abroad

   그들은 함께 _____ 을 하고 있다.
   영화를 보고 있는
   운동하고 있는
   해외여행을 하는

3 What are you doing _____?
   tomorrow | after school | this Friday night

   당신은 _____ 무엇을 할 예정인가요?
   내일 | 방과 후에 | 이번 주 금요일 밤에

Unit **02** What are you doing now?

Let's Read

Magic Words
Being More Polite

When you speak English, always remember the "magic words." These magic words are very important. Here are some magic words:

    Excuse me.
    Please.
    Thank you.

Use these words when you ask people for help or when you need something. If you use these words, you can be more polite. For example, if you need directions from a stranger, there are two ways to ask that person for help:

    Hey, you! Where is Gangnam?
    Excuse me. Where is Gangnam?

If you yell "Hey, you!" to a stranger, he will probably ignore you. But if the first words you say to a stranger are "Excuse me," he will probably help you.

In addition, use the word "please" when you ask for something. "Please" makes a sentence more polite. For example, you could ask:

    Can you help me?
    Can you help me, please?

Both are good expressions, but by using "please," you are being more polite, so the person will be more likely to help you.

Finally, when someone helps you, always say, "Thank you." You can say, "Thank you very much," "Thanks a lot," or "Thanks." You can even say other expressions like "Thank you for helping me." But always remember to thank people. "Thanks" is a great magic word.

Let's Talk More

1. Do you always use "magic words" in English? Why or why not?
2. How do you feel when people don't say "magic words" to you?
3. What are some more "magic words" in English?

UNIT 03 Where is it?

Vocabulary

- I'm lost. 길을 잃었어요.
- look for ~을 찾다
- next to ~의 옆에
- It's straight ahead. 곧장 가면 있어요.
- You can't miss it. 쉽게 찾을 수 있어요.
- Can you tell me how to get to ~?
  ~에 가는 길을 알려 주시겠어요?
- get on (버스, 지하철 등을) 타다
- get off (버스, 지하철 등에서) 내리다
- transfer at ~ ~에서 갈아타다
- go toward ~쪽으로 가다
- stop 정거장
- go out 나가다
- go straight 직진하다
- block 블록, 한 구획
- turn right 우회전하다
- turn left 좌회전하다
- on your right 오른쪽에
- on your left 왼쪽에
- direction 방향

Get Ready — Prepositions of Location

Use prepositions of location to describe where something is.

over / above

under / beneath

on / on top of

in / inside

behind / in back of

around

next to / by / beside

across

between

Conversation 1 — Asking for Directions — Track 08

Listen carefully. Then, practice the following conversation with your partner.

Tourist	Excuse me. I think I'm lost.
Rick	What are you looking for?
Tourist	Where is the shopping center?
Rick	It's next to the supermarket.
Tourist	Great. Um... where's the supermarket located?
Rick	It's straight ahead. You can't miss it.

Focus

A Look at the map. Then, write the correct prepositions in the blanks.

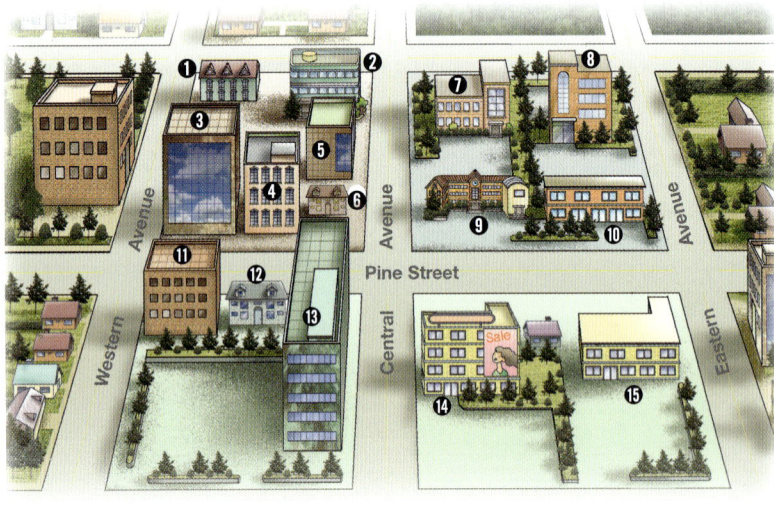

1. music store
2. travel agency
3. culture center
4. bookstore
5. hotel
6. hot dog salesman
7. hospital
8. Burger King
9. school
10. bus station
11. drugstore
12. Korean restaurant
13. department store
14. supermarket
15. gas station

1. The Korean restaurant is _____ Pine Street.
2. The music store is _____ the culture center.
3. The hot dog salesman is _____ the hotel.
4. Burger King is _____ the drugstore.
5. The supermarket is _____ the gas station.
6. The culture center is _____ the hotel.
7. The bookstore is _____ the Korean restaurant.
8. The department store is _____ Pine Street and Central Avenue.

> on
> on the corner of
> next to
> near
> behind
> across from
> far from
> in front of

B Look at the map. Then, answer the questions.

❶ hotel
❷ hospital
❸ rental car agency
❹ library
❺ shopping center
❻ school
❼ office building
❽ bar
❾ park
❿ bookstore
⓫ supermarket
⓬ electronics store
⓭ restaurant

A   Where is the school?
B   The school is on Main Street.

1   Where is the hospital?   _____
2   Where is the supermarket?   _____
3   Where is the library?   _____
4   Where is the bookstore?   _____
5   Where is the shopping center located?   _____
6   Where is the hotel located?   _____
7   Where is the bar located?   _____
8   Where is the restaurant located?   _____

Listen

Listen again. Then, complete the conversation.

Tourist   Excuse me. I think I'm _____ .

Rick   What are you _____ ?

Tourist   Where is the _____ ?

Rick   It's _____ the supermarket.

Tourist   Great. Um... _____ the supermarket _____ ?

Rick   It's _____ . You can't _____ it.

Unit **03** Where is it?   31

Conversation ❷ Giving Directions — Track 09

Listen carefully. Then, practice the following conversation with your partner.

John: How can I get to the supermarket?
Sumi: The supermarket? Go straight two blocks.
John: Okay. After that, what do I do?
Sumi: Turn right. Then, go straight one block.
John: Okay.
Sumi: The supermarket is on your left.
John: Thanks for the directions.

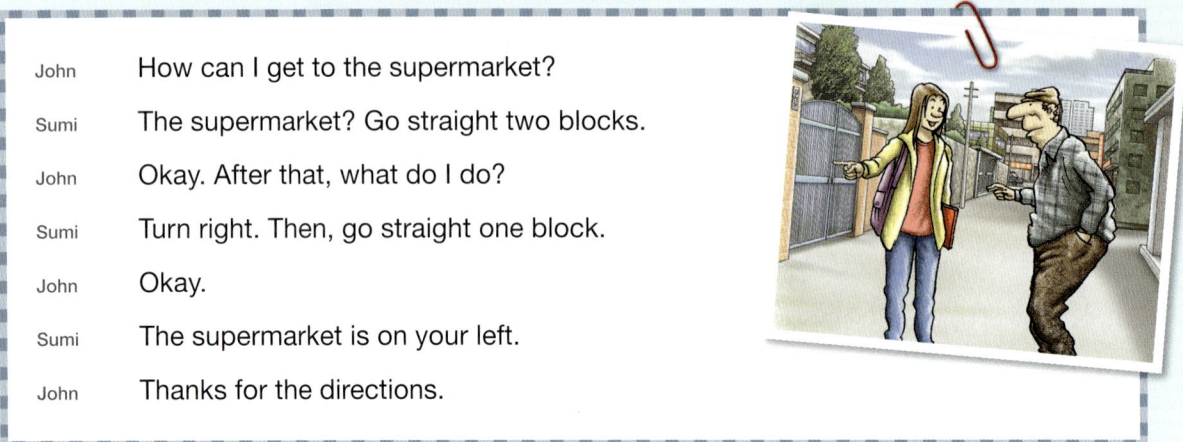

Focus

Look at the map. Then, do the following activities (A & B).

① library
② apartment building
③ post office
④ spa
⑤ Joe's Bar
⑥ supermarket
⑦ swimming pool
⑧ pub
⑨ school
⑩ bakery
⑪ bank
⑫ park
⑬ restaurant
⑭ subway station
⑮ coffee shop

32 English Communication 1

A   Ask your partner for directions.

> A   How can I get to the subway station?
> B   Walk down Oak Street. Turn left on Third Avenue. It's on your right.

1   bank (from Point 1)   2   school (from Point 2)

3   swimming pool (from Point 4)   4   library (from Point 3)

5   post office (from Point 2)   6   supermarket (from Point 4)

7   subway station (from Point 1)   8   apartment building (from Point 3)

B   Answer "true" or "false."

1   The park is next to the supermarket.   _____
2   The post office is on First Avenue.   _____
3   The bank is across from the restaurant.   _____
4   The subway station is on Oak Street.   _____
5   The bakery is near the school.   _____
6   The pub is next to the post office.   _____
7   The library is across from the spa.   _____

Listen

Listen again. Then, complete the conversation.

John   _____ get to the supermarket?

Sumi   The supermarket? Go _____ two blocks.

John   Okay. After that, what do I do?

Sumi   _____. Then, go straight one block.

John   Okay.

Sumi   The supermarket is _____.

John   Thanks for the _____.

Unit 03 Where is it?   33

Conversation 3 — Giving Subway Directions

Track 10

Listen carefully. Then, practice the following conversation with your partner.

John	Can you tell me how to get to Kyobo Bookstore?
Minhee	Sure. We are at Hongik University Station now. Get on the subway toward Sinchon.
John	How many stops should I go?
Minhee	Go 4 stops. After that, transfer at Chungjeongro Station. Go toward Seodaemun Station.
John	Okay.
Minhee	Go 2 stops. Get off at Gwanghwamun Station. Then, go out Exit 2.

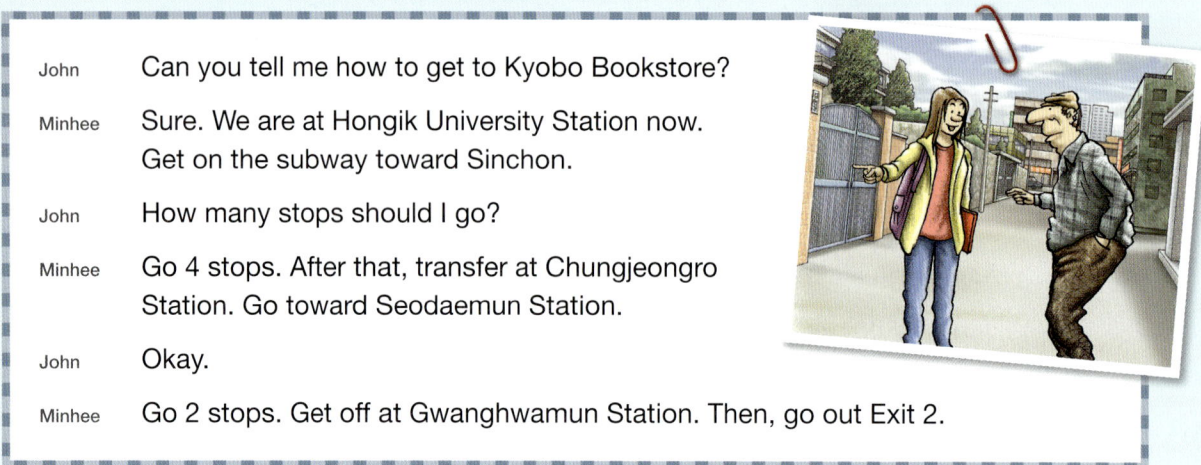

Focus

Look at the subway map. Then, do the following activities (A, B, C, & D).

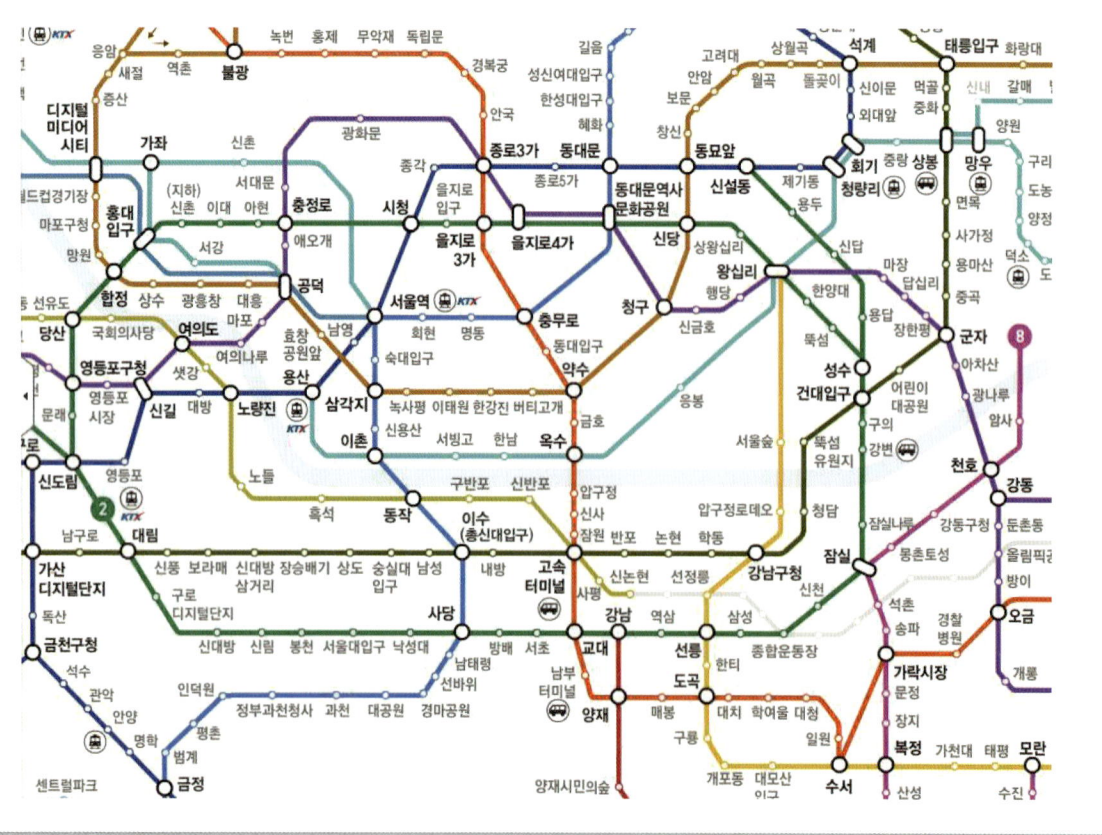

34 English Communication 1

A *Complete the sentences.*

1 It's _____ stops from Sangsu Station to Itaewon Station.

2 It's _____ stops from Sadang Station to Daerim Station.

3 It's _____ stops from Gongduk Station to Gwanghwamun Station.

4 To go from Samsung Station to Yangjae Station, transfer at _____ Station.

5 To go from Songpa Station to Samsung Station, transfer at _____ Station.

6 To go from Sillim Station to Yongsan Station, transfer at _____ Station.

B *Match the expressions to make complete sentences.*

1 It's four stops from   ⓐ transfer at Yaksu Sta.
2 To go from Geumho Sta. to Bomun Sta.,   ⓑ transfer at Oksu Sta.
3 It's two stops from   ⓒ Sadang Sta. to Samgagji Sta.
4 To go from Sillim Sta. to Dongjak Sta.,   ⓓ transfer at Sadang Sta.
5 To go from Apgujeong Sta. to Hannam Sta.,   ⓔ Yangjae Sta. to Dogok Sta.

C *Ask your partner for directions. Then, write the answers.*

1 You are at Seodaemun Station. How can you get to Chungmuro Station?

2 You are at Sinsa Station. How can you get to Namyeong Station?

3 You are at Bangbae Station. How can you get to Daechi Station?

4 You are at Hannam Station. How can you get to Jamsil Station?

5 You are at Sinchon Station. How can you get to Banpo Station?

Listen

Listen again. Then, complete the conversation.

John   Can you tell me _____ Kyobo Bookstore.

Minhee   Sure. We are at Hongik University Station now. _____ the subway toward Sinchon.

John   _____ should I go?

Minhee   Go 4 stops. After that, _____ at Chungjeongro Station. Go _____ Seodaemun Station.

John   Okay.

Minhee   Go 2 stops. _____ at Gwanghwamun Station. Then, go out _____ 2.

Your Turn to Speak

Talk to three other students. Ask them questions. Then, write the answers.

How do you get from ~?

	Student ❶	Student ❷	Student ❸
your home to school			
your home to Seoul Sta.			
your home to Shinchon Sta.			

Let's Practice Pronunciation

Track 11

Pronunciation

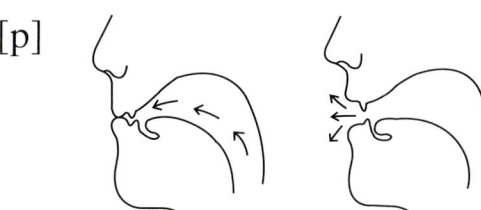
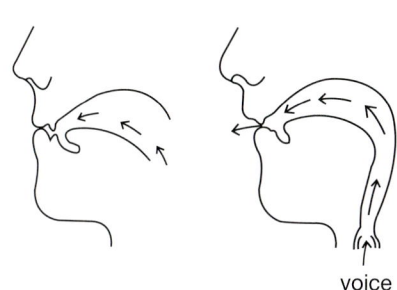

voice

Word Comparison

[p] and [b] have different sounds. Try pronouncing the words below.

[p]	pack	push	pan	pig	cap	lap	tap	rapid	staple
[b]	back	bush	ban	big	cab	lab	tab	rabid	stable

Sentences

Read the following sentences. Try to pronounce [p] and [b] correctly.

1 **Paul** is having a **party** with the **boys**.
2 **Bob blew bubbles by** using **cheap soap**.
3 **Please be** careful to **pack** the **books properly**.
4 What a **big pig** you have!
5 Don't **play** with the **butter**.

Sentence Patterns

1 Where is _____ ?
   the shopping center | your home | the bank

2 The supermarket is _____ .
   on your left | next to the hotel | across from the bank

3 Get off at _____ .
   Gwanghwamun Sta. | Suwon Sta. | the next sta.

_____ 이 어디에 있습니까?
쇼핑센터 | 당신의 집 | 은행

슈퍼마켓은 _____ 에 있습니다.
당신의 왼쪽에 | 호텔 옆에 | 은행 건너편에

_____ 에서 내리세요.
광화문 | 수원역 | 다음역

Let's Read

Giving Directions

Different Directions in the United States and Korea

Giving directions in the United States and Korea can be very different experiences for people. Let's look at how they are different. In the U.S., a person might ask:

> Where is the bank?
> Where is your house?

The answer is often an address. You might say, "The bank is located at 100 Main Street," or "My address is 220 Douglas Drive." It's very common just to give the address. Because most Americans know street names and their locations, it's okay to give the street name and number.

However, giving directions in Korea is very different. Using street names as addresses is not very common in Korea. Instead, people often use landmarks or general locations when giving people directions. For example, in Korea, someone may ask:

> Where is your office?
> Where is the restaurant?

The answer is often NOT an address. Instead, the answer is usually long. You might say, "Go to Sadang Station. Go out Exit 5 and walk straight for 100 meters. The restaurant is on your left." In Korea, you must often give more detailed directions because people don't use addresses very much. However, in the U.S., you can often simply use an address to give directions.

Let's Talk More

1. Can you give directions from school to your house?
2. Do you like to help people when they ask for directions?

UNIT 04 What do you usually do after school?

Vocabulary

- daily schedule 하루 일과
- What time do you ~? 당신은 몇 시에 ~해요?
- wake up 잠에서 깨다
- go to bed 잠자리에 들다
- get dressed 옷을 입다
- go to work 출근하다
- go to school 학교에 가다
- always 항상, 언제나
- usually 보통, 대개
- often 자주
- sometimes 가끔, 때때로
- Do you have any plans? 어떤 계획이 있어요?
- How often do you ~? 얼마나 자주 ~하나요?
- Have a good time. 좋은 시간 보내세요.
- twice a week 일주일에 두 번
- once a year 일년에 한 번
- every morning 매일 아침
- seldom 거의 ~않다
- hardly 거의 ~않다
- never 절대로 ~않다

Get Ready — Prepositions of Time

Use different prepositions with different words.

on	in	at
on December 25	in the afternoon	at 8 o'clock
on Friday	in March	at noon
on Saturday evening	in summer	at midnight
on Valentine's Day	in 1994	at sunset / at sunrise

Write the correct prepositions.

1. _____ June
2. _____ Monday
3. _____ midnight
4. _____ 2015
5. _____ August 31
6. _____ 5 o'clock
7. _____ Sunday morning
8. _____ 11 o'clock
9. _____ spring
10. _____ New Year's Day
11. _____ the morning
12. _____ February

Conversation 1 — Times of Daily Activities

Track 12

Listen carefully. Then, practice the following conversation with your partner.

Sungmin: What do you usually do in the morning?
Rick: I usually wake up at 7. Then, I get dressed.
Sungmin: What time do you go to work?
Rick: I go to work at 9.
Sungmin: Do you work every day?
Rick: No, I don't. I never work on Saturday and Sunday.

Focus

A What's your daily schedule?

What time do you _____?

- wake up
- go to school
- have lunch
- get home
- do your homework
- eat breakfast
- have your first class
- go to work
- have dinner
- go to bed

B Write about yourself.

1. What time do you wake up? — I usually wake up at 6:30.
2. What time do you eat breakfast? _____
3. When do you go to school? _____
4. When do you go to work? _____
5. What time do you stop working? _____
6. What time do you get home? _____
7. When do you have dinner? _____
8. When do you relax at home? _____
9. What time do you watch television? _____
10. When do you go to bed? _____

C *Study the months and dates.*

Months	January	February	March	April	May	June
	July	August	September	October	November	December

Dates					
1st	first	11th	eleventh	21st	twenty-first
2nd	second	12th	twelfth	22nd	twenty-second
3rd	third	13th	thirteenth	23rd	twenty-third
4th	fourth	14th	fourteenth	24th	twenty-fourth
5th	fifth	15th	fifteenth	25th	twenty-fifth
6th	sixth	16th	sixteenth	26th	twenty-sixth
7th	seventh	17th	seventeenth	27th	twenty-seventh
8th	eighth	18th	eighteenth	28th	twenty-eighth
9th	ninth	19th	nineteenth	29th	twenty-ninth
10th	tenth	20th	twentieth	30th / 31st	thirtieth / thirty-first

D *Answer the questions by using the months and dates.*

1. When is Christmas?   It's on December twenty-fifth.
2. When is Valentine's Day?   _____
3. When is New Year's Day?   _____
4. When is Korean Independence Day?   _____
5. When is your birthday?   _____
6. When is your next English class?   _____

Listen

Listen again. Then, complete the conversation.

Sungmin What do you _____ do _____ the morning?

Rick I usually _____ at 7. Then, I _____.

Sungmin _____ do you go to work?

Rick I go to work _____.

Sungmin Do you work _____?

Rick No, I don't. I _____ work _____ Saturday and Saturday.

Conversation 2 — Frequency of Actions

🅞 Track 13

Listen carefully. Then, practice the following conversation with your partner.

Minhee   Do you always have dinner at 6?
Jihye   Yes, I do. What about you?
Minhee   I often have dinner at 6. But I sometimes eat at 7.
Jihye   What do you usually do after dinner?
Minhee   I usually watch TV or read a book.
Jihye   Not me. I always play the piano after dinner.

Focus

A Match the questions with the answers.

1. What time do you usually wake up?
2. What do you usually eat?
3. What do you talk about with your friends?
4. When do you usually have dinner?
5. What do you often do on the weekend?
6. Where do you usually meet your friends?
7. Who do you usually call every day?

ⓐ I always have Korean food.
ⓑ At 6 P.M.
ⓒ We talk about our jobs.
ⓓ I get up at 7 A.M.
ⓔ I usually meet my friends.
ⓕ My parents.
ⓖ At the coffee shop.

B Talk to your partner. Ask and answer the questions.

> A What do you usually do after school?
> B I usually go to the gym after school.

What do you usually _____?

- do after school
- watch on TV
- eat
- talk about with your friends
- do for exercise
- do on the weekend
- read
- cook
- do with your friends
- write about in your diary

42   English Communication 1

C *Read the sentences. Complete the conversation by using the adverbs.*

1 What do you have for breakfast? (usually)
   → <u>What do you usually have for breakfast?</u>

2 I have coffee, scrambled eggs, and pancakes. (often)
   → _____

3 Do you eat breakfast at work? (usually)
   → _____

4 I have breakfast at my desk. (sometimes)
   → _____

5 Do you eat a bowl of rice for breakfast? (usually)
   → _____

6 No, I have rice. (hardly ever)
   → _____

D *Circle the mistakes. Then, write the correct sentences.*

1 Mr. Peters (goes sometimes) to church.   <u>Mr. Peters sometimes goes to church.</u>
2 What do usually you do after school?   _____
3 I brush often my teeth.   _____
4 Lisa studies hard never.   _____
5 Do always you watch action movies?   _____
6 What do they study usually?   _____
7 He always sometimes surfs the Internet.   _____

Listen

Listen again. Then, complete the conversation.

Minhee   Do you _____ have dinner _____ 6?

Jihye   Yes, I do. What about you?

Minhee   I _____ have dinner at 6. But I _____ eat at 7.

Jihye   What do you usually do _____?

Minhee   I _____ watch TV or read a book.

Jihye   Not me. I _____ play the piano after dinner.

Conversation 3 — How Often You Do Something — Track 14

Listen carefully. Then, practice the following conversation with your partner.

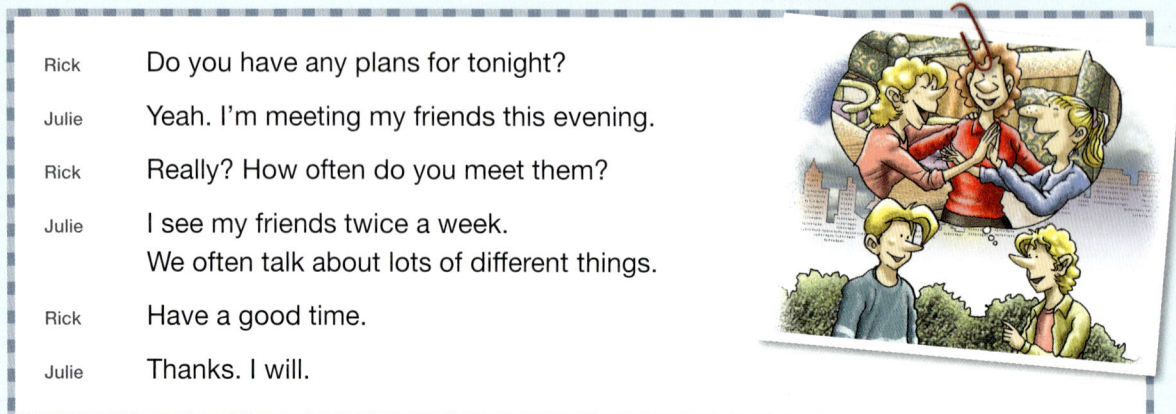

Rick	Do you have any plans for tonight?
Julie	Yeah. I'm meeting my friends this evening.
Rick	Really? How often do you meet them?
Julie	I see my friends twice a week. We often talk about lots of different things.
Rick	Have a good time.
Julie	Thanks. I will.

Focus

A Match the adverbs with the time expressions.

		always	usually	often	sometimes	seldom	never
1	every morning	✓					
2	once a year						
3	once every other week						
4	once a month						
5	twice a month						
6	every Monday						
7	once every 10 years						

B Ask your partner the questions. Then, write the answers.

A	How often do you study English?
B	I study English every day.

1. How often do you watch TV? _____
2. How often do you send text messages? _____
3. How often do you cook? _____
4. How often does your best friend call you? _____
5. How often does your teacher give you homework? _____

C Answer "true" or "false."

1 I cook dinner four times a week. _____
2 My best friend calls me twice a day. _____
3 I study English every day. _____
4 I take a trip three times a year. _____
5 My father goes to work five times a week. _____
6 I meet my friends on the weekend twice a month. _____
7 My family has breakfast together every day. _____
8 I check my email five times a day. _____

D Read the sentences. Change the underlined expressions to adverbs of frequency.

> A He watches TV <u>thirty minutes a day</u>.
> B He sometimes watches TV.

1 John reads the newspaper <u>every day</u>. ➔ _John always reads the newspaper._
2 Sumi takes a trip <u>twice a year</u>. ➔ _____
3 My brother plays soccer <u>once a week</u>. ➔ _____
4 Mr. Park washes his car <u>four times a year</u>. ➔ _____
5 Scott calls his girlfriend <u>twice a day</u>. ➔ _____
6 Ms. Han cooks <u>three times a month</u>. ➔ _____

E Complete the sentences by using adverbs of frequency.

1 I __sometimes__ eat Chinese food.
2 I _____ read comic books.
3 I always _____.
4 I never _____.
5 I _____ play sports.
6 I _____ shop online.
7 My parents sometimes _____.
8 My best friend usually _____.
9 My best friend never _____.
10 My brother/sister often _____.

Listen

Listen again. Then, complete the conversation.

Rick Do you have _____ for tonight?

Julie Yeah. I'm _____ my friends this evening.

Rick Really? _____ do you meet them?

Julie I see my friends _____.
We _____ talk about _____ things.

Rick _____ a good time.

Julie Thanks. I _____.

Your Turn to Speak

Talk to three other students. Ask them questions. Then, write the answers.

How often do you _____?

	Student ❶	Student ❷	Student ❸
exercise			
eat pizza			
meet your friends			
visit the library			

Let's Practice Pronunciation   Track 15

Pronunciation

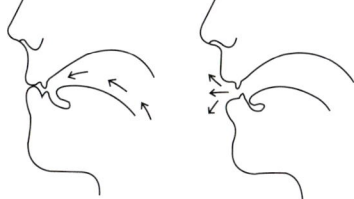

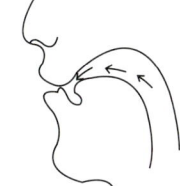

Word Comparison

[p] and [f] have different sounds. Try pronouncing the words below.

[p]	pat	pill	pine	pan	pound	copy	cup	hoop	leap
[f]	fat	fill	fine	fan	found	coffee	cuff	hoof	leaf

Sentences

Read the following sentences. Try to pronounce [p] and [f] correctly.

1 Big **airplanes flew** over the **factories**.
2 A **few puppies followed Patrick for five** minutes.
3 **Figs, plums, pickles,** and **pumpkins** are all **foods**.
4 **People often repeat different expressions**.
5 **Pat** did not **expect** to **sniff powdered pepper**.

Sentence Patterns

1 When do you usually _____ ?
  wake up | leave work | do your homework

  당신은 주로 언제 _____ 하나요?
  일어나다 | 퇴근하다 | 숙제를 하다

2 I _____ study hard.
  always | usually | sometimes

  나는 _____ 공부를 열심히 한다.
  항상 | 보통 | 가끔

3 I go to work _____.
  every day | five days a week | three times a week

  나는 _____ 출근한다.
  매일 | 일주일에 5일 | 일주일에 세 번

Let's Read

Formal and Casual
Using Polite Expressions in English

In Korean, it is very easy to tell when a person is using formal or casual language. The polite expressions are built into the language in the forms of *banmal* and *jondaemal*. But English is different. There are formal and informal expressions in English, but they are not as clear as they are in Korean.

One time to use formal and casual language is when you answer questions. If someone asks you a Yes/No question, you might give a casual answer like this:

Do you like Korean food?	Yes. / Yeah.
Can you swim well?	No. / Nope.

These are good answers, but, depending upon the situation, you might need to be more formal. One way to be formal when answering questions is simply to use complete sentences like this:

Do you like Korean food?	Yes, I do.
Can you swim well?	No, I can't.

When you are speaking with your friends, it's fine to use casual language. But in the classroom, at work, or in other more formal situations, try using formal language in English.

There are many other ways in which English uses casual and formal language. Can you think of any?

Let's Talk More

1. What are some casual words or expressions in English?
2. What are some formal words or expressions in English?
3. Do you prefer formal or casual language? Why?

UNIT 05 Can you tell me about your family?

Vocabulary

- Can you tell me about ~? ~에 대해서 말해 주시겠어요?
- There are ~ people in my family. 우리 가족은 ~명입니다.
- family tree 가계도
- big family 대가족
- small family 소가족
- immediate family 직계가족
- extended family 확대가족
- relative 친척
- job 직업 (= occupation)
- What is your job? 직업이 뭐예요? (= What do you do?)
- work for a company 회사에서 일하다
- housewife 주부
- be in the army 군대에 있다
- study at a university 대학교에서 공부하다
- How old is ~? ~는 몇 살이죠?
- in one's early thirties 30대 초반의
- in one's mid-forties 40대 중반의
- in one's late fifties 50대 후반의

Get Ready

Do you know these words? Discuss these words with your classmates.

Marriage & Divorce
- fiancé / fiancée
- get married
- arranged marriage
- get divorced
- single parent

Family
- live with one's family
- be separated from one's family
- get along well with
- be alike
- henpeck / nag

- immediate family
- extended family
- orphan
- adopt / adoption
- in-laws

Conversation ❶ Talking about Families — Track 16

Listen carefully. Then, practice the following conversation with your partner.

Julie	Can you tell me about your family?
John	There are five people in my family: my mother, father, brother, sister, and me.
Julie	Is your brother older or younger than you?
John	He is older than me. And my sister is younger than me.
Julie	I have an older sister and two younger brothers.
John	Wow! That's a big family.

Focus

A *Look at the family tree.*

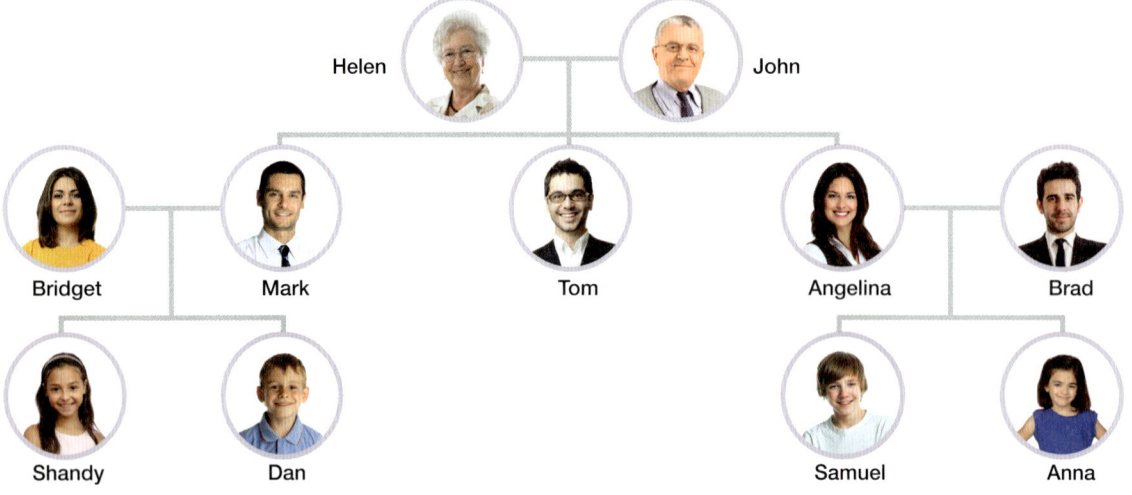

Immediate Family (직계가족)

Mark is Bridget's **husband** and Shandy and Dan's **father**.

Bridget is Mark's **wife** and Shandy and Dan's **mother**.

Mark and Bridget are Shandy and Dan's **parents**.

Shandy is Mark and Bridget's **daughter**. Dan is their **son**.

Shandy is Dan's **sister**. Dan is Shandy's **brother**.

Extended Family (확대 가족)

Helen is Shandy and Dan's **grandmother**. John is their **grandfather**.

Helen and John are Shandy and Dan's **grandparents**.

Shandy is Helen and John's **granddaughter**. Dan is their **grandson**.

Tom and Brad are Shandy and Dan's **uncles**.

Angelina is Shandy and Dan's **aunt**.

Shandy is Tom, Angelina, and Brad's **niece**. Dan is their **nephew**.

Samuel and Anna are Shandy and Dan's **cousins**.

Bridget is Helen and John's **daughter-in-law**. Brad is their **son-in-law**.

B *Complete the sentences by using the words in the box.*

1. Angelina is Samuel and Anna's _____.
2. Samuel is Brad's _____.
3. Brad is Samuel's _____.
4. Angelina and Brad are Samuel and Anna's _____.
5. Tom and Mark are Samuel's _____.
6. Bridget is Samuel and Anna's _____.
7. Anna is Helen and John's _____.
8. Samuel is Tom's _____.
9. Anna is Dan's _____.
10. Shandy and Anna are Tom's _____.

C *Answer the questions.*

1. What's your father's name?   His name is _____.
2. What's your mother's name?   Her name is _____.
3. How many brothers and sisters do you have?   I have _____.
4. Is your brother older or younger than you?   _____.
5. Is your sister older or younger than you?   _____.
6. Tell me about your uncles and aunts.   I have _____.
7. Who is your favorite relative?   My favorite relative is _____.
8. How many cousins do you have?   I have _____.

Listen

Listen again. Then, complete the conversation.

Julie   Can you _____ your family?

John   There are _____ people in my family: my mother, father, brother, sister, and me.

Julie   Is your brother _____ or _____ than you?

John   He is _____ me. And my sister is _____ me.

Julie   I have an _____ and two _____.

John   Wow! That's a _____.

Conversation 2 — Family Members' Jobs

Track 17

Listen carefully. Then, practice the following conversation with your partner.

Sungmin: What does your father do?

Sumi: He works for a company. What is your father's job?

Sungmin: My father teaches at a school. And my mom is a housewife.

Sumi: What about your brother and sister?

Sungmin: My brother is in the army, but my sister studies at a university.

Sumi: I'm an only child. I don't have any brothers or sisters.

Focus

A *Match the jobs with their descriptions.*

1. A teacher
2. An office worker
3. A doctor
4. A programmer
5. A receptionist
6. A police officer
7. A civil servant
8. An architect

ⓐ works for the government.
ⓑ protects civilians and catches criminals.
ⓒ designs houses and buildings.
ⓓ works at a school and instructs students.
ⓔ answers telephones and greets visitors.
ⓕ uses computers and makes computer programs.
ⓖ works for a company.
ⓗ takes care of sick people.

B *Answer the questions.*

1. What does an athlete do?   _An athlete plays sports._
2. What does a nurse do?   _____
3. What does a professor do?   _____
4. What does a firefighter do?   _____
5. What does an artist do?   _____
6. What does a businessperson do?   _____

C *Look at the job descriptions. Then, choose the right words from the box.*

| lawyer | maid | plumber | congressman | secretary | taxi driver |

1 My job duties include typing letters, answering the phone, keeping records, and scheduling meetings. I sometimes make coffee for my boss. _____

2 I work in bathrooms and kitchens. I fix leaky pipes and unclog drains. _____

3 I drive for a living. I pick up passengers and take them where they want to go. I usually know where every place in the city is. _____

4 I represent people in court, and I am very knowledgeable about the law. My job is to prove my client's innocence. _____

5 I usually work for rich people. I do their laundry, wash their dishes, and cook. I sometimes run errands. _____

6 I'm an elected official. My job is to represent ordinary citizens. I have the power to create new laws. _____

D *Complete the sentences by using the words in the box. Change the forms of the words.*

Present Simple Tense Statements

I **walk** to school.	I **don't study** every day.
You **ride** your bike to school.	You **don't live** near here.
He **works** near here.	He **doesn't work** downtown.
She **takes** the bus to work.	She **doesn't drive** to work.
We **live** with our parents.	We **don't own** a dog.
They **use** public transportation.	They **don't need** a car.

* don't = do not / doesn't = does not

| ride | sell | help | go | be | have | work | cook |

1 My sister _____ to high school.

2 Her father _____ at an engineering company.

3 John's mother _____ a housewife.

4 She _____ one younger brother and two older sisters.

5 Sumi _____ her aunt wash the dishes.

6 Joe _____ his bicycle in the park every morning.

7 Tina _____ clothes at a department store.

8 That chef _____ food at a restaurant.

E *Complete the sentences with the correct verb forms.*

1. My family and I (live / lives) in the suburbs. My wife and I (work / works) near here, so we (walk / walks) to work. Our son (don't / doesn't) drive. He (ride / rides) his bike to school.

2. My parents (live / lives) in the city. My mother (take / takes) the train to work. My father is retired, so he (don't / doesn't) work now. He also (use / uses) public transportation, so he (don't / doesn't) need a car.

Listen

Listen again. Then, complete the conversation.

Sungmin	What _____ your father _____?
Sumi	He _____ a company.
	What is your father's job?
Sungmin	My father _____ at a school.
	And my mom is a _____.
Sumi	What about your brother and sister?
Sungmin	My brother is _____, but my sister _____.
Sumi	I'm an _____. I don't have any brothers or sisters.

Your Turn to Speak

Talk to three other students. Ask them questions. Then, write the answers.

A: What does your father do?
B: He is a salesman.

	Student ❶	Student ❷	Student ❸
father			
mother			
brother / sister			

54 English Communication 1

Conversation 3 — Talking about Age — Track 18

Listen carefully. Then, practice the following conversation with your partner.

Minhee	How old is your brother?
Rick	My brother is twenty-five years old.
Minhee	Hmm. My sister is thirty.
Rick	What about your parents?
Minhee	My parents are in their late fifties.
Rick	How about you?
Minhee	Sorry. That's top secret!

Focus

A Look at the pictures. Then, complete the sentences.

in her twenties	in her mid-forties	in her seventies
in her teens	in his early thirties	in his late fifties

❶
She's _____.

❷
She's _____.

❸
He's _____.

❹
She's _____.

❺
He's _____.

❻
She's _____.

B *Answer "true" or "false."*

1 Eric is twenty-three years old. He's in his late twenties.   _____
2 Minho is twelve. He's a teenager.   _____
3 Mr. Kim is thirty years old. He's in his early thirties.   _____
4 Sumi's grandmother is seventy-seven. She's elderly.   _____
5 Miyoung is fifty-nine years old. She's in her mid-fifties.   _____
6 I'm in my twenties.   _____

Listen

Listen again. Then, complete the conversation.

Minhee	_____ is your brother?
Rick	My brother is _____.
Minhee	Hmm. My sister is _____.
Rick	What about your parents?
Minhee	My parents are in their _____.
Rick	How about you?
Minhee	Sorry. That's _____!

Your Turn to Speak

Talk to three other students. Ask them questions. Then, write the answers.

A How old is your father?
B He is in his late fifties.

	Student ❶	Student ❷	Student ❸
father			
mother			
grandparents			

Let's Practice Pronunciation

Track 19

Pronunciation

[b]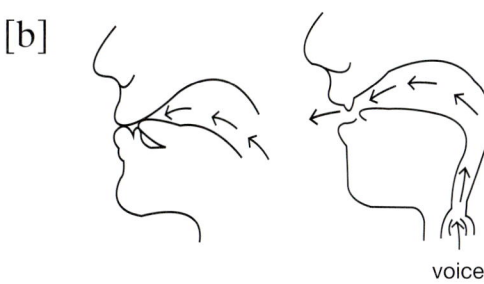
voice

[v]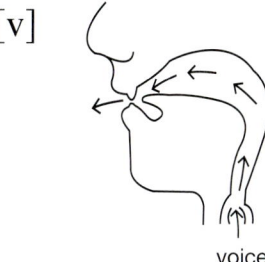
voice

Word Comparison

[b] and [v] have different sounds. Try pronouncing the words below.

[b]	ban	bend	bent	bat	best	fiber	curb	labor	marble
[v]	van	vend	vent	vat	vest	fiver	curve	laver	marvel

Sentences

Read the following sentences. Try to pronounce [b] and [v] correctly.

1 **Save** the **best** for last.
2 **Buy** tickets in **advance**.
3 **Everyone loved** the **bride's beautiful veil**.
4 The **starving baby grabbed** a **banana** and **gobbled** it down.
5 Put a **veil over** the **bale**.

Sentence Patterns

1 There are _____ people in my family.   나의 가족은 _____ 명이다.
   five | seven | only three   다섯 명 | 일곱 명 | 딱 세 명

2 My father _____.   우리 아버지는 _____.
   works at a company   회사에서 일한다
   teaches at a school   학교에서 가르친다
   owns a restaurant   식당을 소유하고 있다

3 How old is _____?   _____는 몇 살이니?
   your mother | your sister | your best friend   너의 어머니 | 너의 언니 | 너의 가장 친한 친구

Let's Read

Job Descriptions
Giving Longer Answers

When someone asks, "What's your job?" you can give an easy answer like, "I'm an office worker," "I'm a teacher," or "I'm a civil servant." These are all perfectly good answers.

However, in American culture, when a person asks you a question and you give a short answer, you are implying that you don't want to speak with him or her. So in this case, giving long answers has a cultural importance. For example, don't just say, "I'm a teacher." Instead, you can say:

> I'm a teacher at Seoul High School.
> I teach math at a middle school.
> I'm a third grade teacher at Jongro Elementary School.

Or don't just say, "I'm an office worker." Instead, you can say:

> I'm an office worker at Samsung Engineering.
> I'm a businesswoman. I work for LG.
> I'm a manager at Hyundai Securities.

When you give very short answers, Americans often think that you don't want to talk to them, so they will stop asking questions. To avoid any misunderstandings, you should give longer answers with more information. Then, the person will understand that you want to continue the conversation.

Let's Talk More

1. Do you often give short answers or long answers? Why?
2. What do you think when a person only gives short answers?

UNIT 06 What do you like?

Vocabulary

- Let's ~ ~하자
- go into ~ ~로 들어가다
- pet store 애완동물 가게
- Do you like ~? 당신은 ~을 좋아하나요?
- I like ~ very much. 나는 ~을 무척 좋아해요.
- I like ~ more. 나는 ~을 더 좋아해요.
- What kind of ~ do you like? 어떤 종류의 ~을 좋아해요?
- Which do you prefer, A or B? A와 B중 어느 것을 좋아해요?
- love 아주 좋아하다
- be crazy about ~ ~을 아주 좋아하다, ~에 푹 빠져 있다
- hate 싫어하다
- can't stand (참을 수 없을 정도로) 싫다
- Let me guess. 내가 맞춰 볼게요.

Get Ready

Work with a partner. Ask and answer questions about likes and dislikes. Use the answers in the box.

Do you like _____?

basketball	keeping yourself busy
rap music	singing
hamburgers	getting up early
coffee	Chinese food
pizza	rainy days
soju	TV dramas
the president	living in Seoul
your boss	watching movies
baseball	eating out

Yes, I love it. / I really like it. / I'm crazy about it. / I kind of like it.
No, I can't stand it. / I dislike it. / I hate it. / I don't like it. / I don't care for it.

Conversation 1 — Talking about Likes

Track 20

Listen carefully. Then, practice the following conversation with your partner.

Minhee	Let's go into that pet store. I love animals.
Sungmin	Really? Do you like dogs or cats?
Minhee	Dogs. I like dogs very much.
Sungmin	What kind of dogs do you like?
Minhee	I think Yorkshire terriers are the best.
Sungmin	They're okay. But I like retrievers more.

Focus

A Write the answers.

A	Do you like cats or dogs?	B	I like cats.
A	Which do you prefer, cats or dogs?	B	I prefer cats.

1　Do you like buses or subways?　　_____
2　Do you like sports or computer games?　_____
3　Which do you prefer, books or movies?　_____
4　Which do you prefer, Korean food or Chinese food?　_____

B Check what you like the most. Then, answer the questions.

What kind of _____ do you like?	
movies	romantic movies, horror movies, comedies, action movies, westerns, musicals, family movies, adventure movies
books	novels, detective stories, fairy tales, comic books, fantasy books, nonfiction books
sports	soccer, baseball, American football, golf, tennis, swimming, skiing
TV programs	soap operas, sitcoms, documentaries, sports, news
music	pop music, rock music, classical music, jazz, hip-hop, dance music

1 What kind of movies do you like?   I like _____.
2 What kind of books do you like?   I like _____.
3 What kind of sports do you like?   I like _____.
4 What kind of TV programs do you usually watch?   I usually watch _____.
5 What kind of music do you usually listen to?   I usually listen to _____.

Listen

Listen again. Then, complete the conversation.

Minhee	Let's go into that _____. I love animals.
Sungmin	Really? _____ dogs _____ cats?
Minhee	Dogs. I like dogs _____.
Sungmin	_____ dogs do you like?
Minhee	I think Yorkshire terriers are _____.
Sungmin	They're okay. But I like retrievers _____.

Your Turn to Speak

Talk to three other students. Ask them questions. Then, write the answers.

A What kind of <u>music</u> do you like?
B I like country music.

	Student ❶	Student ❷	Student ❸
music			
movies			
books			
pets			
snacks			

Conversation 2 — Talking about Favorite Activities

○ Track 21

Listen carefully. Then, practice the following conversation with your partner.

Tom	Why are you so excited today?
Jihye	I'm going to watch a movie with my boyfriend.
Tom	That sounds like fun. I like watching movies.
Jihye	We're also going to my favorite restaurant.
Tom	What kind of food do you like to eat?
Jihye	I love eating Italian food. It's so delicious.

Focus

A What do you like doing? Answer the questions.

1. What do you like doing after school? — I like hanging out with my friends.
2. What do you like to do on the weekend?
3. What do you like doing with your friends?
4. What do you like to eat?
5. Where do you like going on vacation?
6. Where do you like to go after work?
7. Who do you like meeting on the weekend?
8. What kind of person do you like to date?

B Change the following sentences. Use "love" and "be crazy about" instead of "like" and "like very much."

1. Sumi likes watching comedies. — Sumi loves watching comedies.
2. Mr. Lee likes computer games very much. — Mr. Lee is crazy about computer games.
3. David likes to drive his car.
4. The students like English very much.
5. Miss Kim likes going on trips.
6. Larry likes to play sports very much.
7. The children like drawing pictures a lot.
8. I like to shop online very much.

C *Fill in the blanks. Put the verbs in the blanks in their -ing forms.*

Sunny and her family love ____going____ (go) to the park in the spring. They like (1) _____ (have) picnics and love (2) _____ (sit) on the grass. Sunny's mother hates (3) _____ (make) *kimbap*, so her father always makes it instead. Sunny and her brother love (4) _____ (play) with a ball in the park. Sunny's mother likes (5) _____ (lie) on a mat and loves (6) _____ (read) her favorite books. Sunny loves (7) _____ (listen) to classical music, and her brother likes (8) _____ (watch) the people in the park. Sunny's family enjoys (9) _____ (visit) the park because they love (10) _____ (be) outdoors.

D *Circle the incorrect parts. Then, write the correct answers.*

1. Jason loves (play) computer games. — *Jason loves playing computer games.*
2. Mr. and Mrs. Taylor likes driving their car. _____
3. I like to watching sports on television. _____
4. The students like very much doing homework. _____
5. He is crazy his girlfriend. _____
6. Chris likes go out with his friends. _____
7. Mr. Park loving his wife very much. _____
8. I am like my job very much. _____
9. Wendy is about crazy her new puppy. _____
10. Do you liking buying new clothes? _____

Listen

Listen again. Then, complete the conversation.

Tom: Why are you _____ today?

Jihye: I'm going to watch a movie with my boyfriend.

Tom: That sounds like fun. I like _____.

Jihye: We're also going to my _____.

Tom: _____ do you like to eat?

Jihye: I love _____ Italian food. It's so _____.

Conversation ③ Talking about Dislikes

🔘 Track 22

Listen carefully. Then, practice the following conversation with your partner.

Tom	Are you okay? You didn't eat much at lunch today.
Minhee	I don't like hamburgers. So I didn't eat anything.
Tom	Oh. I didn't know that.
Minhee	Yeah. And now it's time to work again.
Tom	Let me guess... You don't like working?
Minhee	Exactly! I can't stand my boss!

Focus

A *Answer the questions.*

A	What animal do you not like?	B	I don't like snakes.
A	What animal do you dislike?	B	I dislike snakes.

1. What class do you not like? _____
2. What song do you dislike? _____
3. What kind of music do you not like? _____
4. What kind of food do you dislike? _____
5. What TV program do you not like? _____

B *Answer the questions.*

A	What food do you hate?	B	I hate noodles.
A	What food can you not stand?	B	I cannot stand noodles.

1. What sport do you hate? _____
2. What movie can you not stand? _____
3. Who do you hate? _____
4. What kind of person can you not stand? _____
5. What subject do you hate? _____

C Look at the example. Then, write similar questions and answers.

> the girls / eat pizza
> (like) ___Do the girls like eating pizza?___
> (yes, love) ___Yes, they love eating pizza.___

1 Sally / drive her car

   (like) _____

   (no, hate) _____

2 Bob and Steve / eat fried chicken

   (like) _____

   (yes, like) _____

3 Mr. Lee / clean the house

   (like) _____

   (no, not like) _____

4 the baby / take medicine

   (like) _____

   (no, hate) _____

5 the children / watch TV

   (like) _____

   (yes, like) _____

6 Kate / do her homework

   (like) _____

   (no, dislike) _____

7 Sam / get up early

   (like) _____

   (no, hate) _____

Listen

Listen again. Then, complete the conversation.

Tom   Are you okay? You didn't _____ at lunch today.

Minhee   I don't like hamburgers. So I _____ anything.

Tom   Oh. I didn't know that.

Minhee   Yeah. And now it's _____ work again.

Tom   Let me guess... You don't like working?

Minhee   Exactly! I _____ my boss!

Your Turn to Speak

Talk to three other students. Ask them questions. Then, write the answers.

A: What <u>animal</u> do you dislike?
B: I dislike cats.

	Student ❶	Student ❷	Student ❸
animal			
song			
kind of movie			
kind of person			

Let's Practice Pronunciation

Track 23

Pronunciation

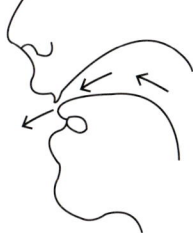
[θ]

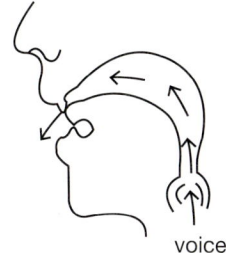
[ð]
voice

Word Comparison

[θ] and [ð] have different sounds. Try pronouncing the words below.

[θ]	theme	faith	wreath	thigh	tooth	thin	ether	thirty	thorn
[ð]	this	father	worthy	they	bathe	thy	other	though	those

Sentences

Read the following sentences. Try to pronounce [θ] and [ð] correctly.

1 I **loathe both** of **them**.
2 **They threw the** cats into **the bathtub**.
3 She is **thinner than** he is.
4 **Three thieves threatened** Mr. **Roth**.
5 **Both** my **father** and **mother** are fifty-**three**.

Sentence Patterns

1 I like _____ very much.
   dogs | sports | my job

   나는 _____ 을 아주 좋아해.
   개 | 스포츠 | 내 일

2 What kind of _____ do you like?
   movies | person | activities

   어떤 종류의 _____ 을 좋아합니까?
   영화 | 사람 | 활동

3 She can't stand _____.
   snakes | cooking | soft drinks

   그녀는 _____ 을 무척 싫어해요.
   뱀 | 요리 | 탄산음료

Let's Read

Strong Expressions
Talking about Loving and Hating

Americans often use strong expressions to talk about likes and dislikes. They often use words like "love" and "hate" to do this. For example, a person might say:

> I love my friends.
> I hate my brother's dog.

Of course, you don't really love your friends; you simply like them very much. And you probably don't hate your brother's dog (unless it always bites you); you are probably just angry at the dog for something that it did. So don't misunderstand people when they use words like "love" and "hate." They just have a very strong sense of like or dislike – not true love or real hate.

In addition, you can use the word "love" to give compliments to people. People always love hearing expressions like this:

> I love your dress. It looks beautiful.
> I love your cooking. This food is delicious.
> I love my English teacher. His class is so much fun.

Listen for people to use "love" and "hate" when they are speaking English. Then, try using these words when you speak English.

Let's Talk More

1. What do you love? What do you hate?
2. Are you surprised when people use strong words like "love" and "hate"?
3. Do you know some other strong expressions? What are they?

UNIT 07 What's he like?

Vocabulary

- **get a date** 데이트하다
- **That's too bad.** 안됐다.
- **introduce A to B** A를 B에게 소개하다
- **What is she like?** 그녀는 어떤 사람이에요?
- **personality** 인격, 사람됨
- **shy** 수줍음을 타는, 내성적인
- **Tell me about ~** ~에 대해서 얘기해 주세요.
- **He is a/an ~ person.** 그는 ~한 사람이에요.
- **outgoing** 사교성이 풍부한
- **make friends** 친구를 사귀다
- **tell jokes** 농담을 하다
- **polite** 예의 바른, 공손한
- **should** ~하는 게 좋다
- **need to** ~할 필요가 있다
- **stop smoking** 담배를 끊다
- **habit** 습관
- **I'm not all bad.** 난 그렇게 나쁜 사람은 아니야.

Get Ready

Discuss these questions.

A   When do you feel nervous?
B   I feel nervous when I take a test.

1 What do you do to calm down?
2 What drives you crazy?
3 What makes you happy?
4 How do you cheer up a friend who's feeling blue?
5 When are you in a good mood?
6 When are you in a bad mood?
7 How do you change your mood?
8 How do you relieve your stress?

Conversation 1 — Talking about Personalities — Track 24

Listen carefully. Then, practice the following conversation with your partner.

Sungmin	I can never get a date.
Jina	That's too bad. I can introduce you to my friend.
Sungmin	Really? What is she like?
Jina	She's great. She's very smart, too.
Sungmin	Does your friend have a good personality?
Jina	She's a little shy, but she's really kind.

Focus

A *Match the personalities with the actions.*

1. impatient
2. polite
3. shy
4. outgoing
5. unselfish
6. energetic
7. reliable
8. angry

ⓐ Sumi always says "please" and "thank you."
ⓑ Lisa is talkative and has many friends.
ⓒ Minho always keeps his promises.
ⓓ Jinhee always shares with other people.
ⓔ Rick doesn't like waiting for people.
ⓕ Nancy gets mad very often.
ⓖ Mark is quiet and doesn't talk to many people.
ⓗ Susan plays many different sports.

B *Describe your personality.*

Are you _____?

- shy or outgoing _____
- funny or serious _____
- happy or sad _____
- selfish or unselfish _____
- careful or careless _____
- energetic or lazy _____
- quiet or talkative _____
- polite or rude _____
- angry or calm _____
- patient or impatient _____
- reliable or unreliable _____
- warm or cold _____

C *Answer the questions.*

1 Are you shy or outgoing? I'm _____.
2 Are you quiet or talkative? _____
3 Are you a funny or serious person? I'm a _____ person.
4 Are you an angry or calm person? _____
5 Do you think you are selfish or unselfish? I think I'm _____.
6 Do you think you are patient or impatient? _____
7 Is your best friend energetic or lazy? He/She is _____.
8 Is your best friend warm or cold? _____

Listen

Listen again. Then, complete the conversation.

Sungmin I can never get date.
Jina That's too bad. I can _____ you to my friend.
Sungmin Really? What _____ she _____?
Jina She's _____. She's very _____, too.
Sungmin Does your friend have a good _____?
Jina She's a little _____, but she's really _____.

Your Turn to Speak

Talk to three other students. Ask them questions. Then, write the answers.

Are you _____?

	Student ❶	Student ❷	Student ❸
shy or outgoing			
patient or impatient			
careful or careless			
energetic or lazy			

Conversation 2 — Explaining Someone's Personality

Track 25

Listen carefully. Then, practice the following conversation with your partner.

Sungmin: Tell me about your boyfriend.
Jihye: Well, he's an outgoing person.
Sungmin: How is he outgoing?
Jihye: He makes friends easily. And he always tells jokes.
Sungmin: Is he also a polite man?
Jihye: Yes, he is. He always opens doors for me.

Focus

A *Match the personality words with their opposites.*

1	angry	_g_	ⓐ	outgoing
2	careful	____	ⓑ	serious
3	energetic	____	ⓒ	rude
4	funny	____	ⓓ	impatient
5	happy	____	ⓔ	unreliable
6	patient	____	ⓕ	sad
7	polite	____	ⓖ	calm
8	quiet	____	ⓗ	lazy
9	reliable	____	ⓘ	careless
10	selfish	____	ⓙ	cold
11	shy	____	ⓚ	talkative
12	warm	____	ⓛ	unselfish

B Complete the sentences with the correct prepositions. Some questions can have two or more answers.

| at | about | in | by | of | with |

1 Are you angry _____ your boyfriend again?
2 Becky was jealous _____ her friend's new car.
3 The students are tired _____ studying grammar.
4 Tina was excited _____ winning the lottery.
5 The teacher wasn't happy _____ the students' grades.
6 My mother was disappointed _____ my bad behavior.
7 Scott is nervous _____ his interview today.
8 Melanie was embarrassed _____ spilling coffee on her T-shirt.

Listen

Listen again. Then, complete the conversation.

Sungmin Tell me about your boyfriend.
Jihye Well, he's an _____.
Sungmin How is he _____?
Jihye He _____ easily. And he always _____.
Sungmin Is he also a _____ man?
Jihye Yes, he is. He always opens doors for me.

Your Turn to Speak

Talk to three other students. Ask them questions. Then, write the answers.

A How are you <u>polite</u>?
B I always say "please" and "thank you."

	Student ❶	Student ❷	Student ❸
polite			
patient			
careless			

Conversation 3 — Talking about Habits

🔘 Track 26

Listen carefully. Then, practice the following conversation with your partner.

Julie You should stop smoking.
Rick   Yeah. It's a bad habit.
Julie You have a lot of bad habits.
Rick   I know. I need to exercise more.
Julie And you should be nicer to people.
Rick   Hey! I'm not all bad!

Focus

A Write "good" or "bad" next to each habit.

1. I exercise and play sports every day.   _good_
2. John loves eating candy and chocolate.   _____
3. Susan wakes up late every day.   _____
4. Minhee eats lots of fruits and vegetables.   _____
5. He smokes two packs of cigarettes a day.   _____
6. James never cleans his room.   _____
7. She often forgets to do her homework.   _____
8. They have excellent manners.   _____

B Complete the sentences. Use the words from the box.

embarrassed	depressed	lonely	anxious
exhausted	jealous	shocked	disgusted

1. Minhee has a new boyfriend, but Jinhee is single. Jinhee is _____ of Minhee.
2. Kevin is _____ because he failed his math test. He is really upset now.
3. James is really _____ since he doesn't have any friends.
4. Eunyoung looks _____. She works too much, so she's very tired.
5. Miss Kim was _____ when she won the lottery. She was completely surprised.

6   I'm _____ by your behavior. Don't ever be rude like that again.

7   Joe is waiting for a call from the company. He's _____ about finding a job.

8   Minho was _____ when he didn't know the answer. Everyone laughed at him.

C *Look at the forms below and practice them.*

> **should + verb**
> Say **should** when something is a good idea but is not required.
>
> **need to + verb**
> Say **need to** when something is a good idea but is not required.
> **Need to** is stronger than **should**.

D *These people have bad habits. How can they change them?*

1   Mr. Kim smokes a lot.   →   He should _____*stop smoking.*_____
2   They drink beer every night.   →   They should _____.
3   Mary weighs too much.   →   She needs to _____.
4   Peter always goes to bed late.   →   He needs to _____.
5   Miss Lee never smiles.   →   She _____.
6   Greg talks too much.   →   He _____.
7   William is very rude.   →   He _____.
8   Mimi often gets angry.   →   She _____.

E *Complete the sentences. Use either "should" or "need to."*

1   I'm hungry. I _____ eat something soon.
2   People _____ eat every day.
3   I have a test in ten minutes. I _____ go to my classroom right now.
4   Scott looks tired. He _____ go to bed early.
5   We _____ watch a movie this weekend.
6   Deb's father just called her. She _____ go home right now.
7   Where _____ we go after school?
8   We _____ study hard, or we won't get good grades.
9   You _____ be nice to your friends.
10 I found a wallet on the ground. What _____ I do?

Listen

Listen again. Then, complete the conversation

Julie   You should _____.

Rick   Yeah. It's a _____.

Julie   You have a lot of bad habits.

Rick   I know. I _____ more.

Julie   And you should _____ to people.

Rick   Hey! I'm not all bad!

Your Turn to Speak

Talk to three other students. Ask them questions. Then, write the answers.

A What do you need to do <u>every day</u>?
B I need to go to school every day.

	Student ❶	Student ❷	Student ❸
every day			
tonight			
tomorrow			
this weekend			

Let's Practice Pronunciation

Track 27

Pronunciation

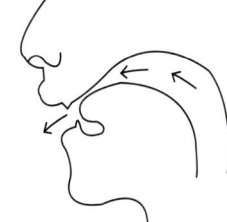
[s]

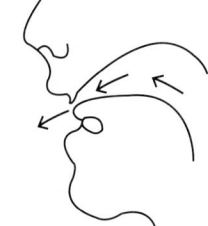
[θ]

Word Comparison

[s] and [θ] have different sounds. Try pronouncing the words below.

[s]	sin	sick	saw	pass	miss	mouse	sank	worse
[θ]	thin	thick	thaw	path	myth	mouth	thank	worth

Sentences

Read the following sentences. Try to pronounce [s] and [θ] correctly.

1. The **box** contained **soap**, **salt**, and other **things**.
2. The **thief stole** the **dress**.
3. The **sea seemed safe** for the moment.
4. Let's **think** positively about the **therapy**.
5. These **things** are **sometimes so tedious**.

Sentence Patterns

1. What is _____ like?　　　　_____ 는 어떻게 생겼습니까?
   she | your sister | Rick　　　　　그녀 | 네 여동생 | 릭

2. She's a/an _____ person.　　그녀는 _____ 한 사람입니다.
   outgoing | polite | kind　　　　　사교적인 | 예의바른 | 친절한

3. He should _____ .　　　　그는 _____ 하는 게 좋습니다.
   stop smoking | be friendly | smile sometimes　　금연하다 | 상냥하다 | 가끔 웃다

Unit **07** What's he like?　**77**

Let's Read

"Should" and "Need To"
A Good Idea vs. an Obligation

Be careful when you use the expressions "should + verb" and "need to + verb." These expressions simply mean that something is a good idea to do. However, you do NOT have to do it. It is NOT 100% required. For example, you might say:

> I'm too angry. I should be calm.
> I weigh too much. I need to lose weight.

For the first sentence, you don't have to be calm. Of course, it's better to be calm than angry, right? And for the second sentence, you don't have to lose weight. But it's probably a good idea to lose weight, right?

We also often use "should + verb" when asking questions. The most common question is "What should I do?" For example, you could say:

> A: I have a test tomorrow. What should I do?
> B: You should study now. You shouldn't update your homepage.

OR

> A: I had a fight with my friend. What should I do?
> B: You need to apologize. You should not fight with him.

Be careful when you use these because the meanings in English are very different. If you use them incorrectly, people will misunderstand you. So always try to use these expressions correctly.

Let's Talk More

1. What are some things you should do?
2. What are some things you need to do?
3. How do you feel when someone misunderstands you?

UNIT 08 What does she look like?

Vocabulary

- What does she look like? 그녀는 어떻게 생겼어요?
- look 외모
- average height 보통 키
- average looking 평범한 외모
- pretty 예쁜
- handsome 잘생긴
- ugly 못생긴
- straight hair 직모
- curly hair 곱슬머리
- spiked hair 끝을 뾰족하게 세운 머리
- ponytail 뒤에서 묶은 머리
- work out 운동하다
- overweight 과체중의, 너무 살찐
- in shape 건강이 좋은, 날씬한
- out of shape 건강이 나쁜, 몸매가 엉망인
- go out 외출하다, 나가다
- wear (옷을) 입다
- clothes 옷
- pants 바지
- dress shirt 와이셔츠

Get Ready

Look at the pictures. What do the people look like?

He is tall.

She is pretty.

She has short hair.

He's average looking.

She has long hair.

He's handsome.

Unit 08 What does she look like?   79

Conversation 1 Looks

Track 28

Listen carefully. Then, practice the following conversation with your partner.

Rick	I have a new girlfriend.
Minhee	That's great. What does she look like?
Rick	She's really pretty. And she has long black hair.
Minhee	Wow! How tall is she?
Rick	She's average height.
Minhee	I'd like to meet her sometime.

Focus

A Look at the pictures and practice the expressions.

He's short.

She's average height.

He's tall.

He's handsome.

He's average looking.

He looks ugly.

She has short hair.

She has long, straight hair.

She has medium-length, curly hair.

He has spiked hair.

She has a ponytail.   She has pigtails.   She has wavy hair.   He is bald.

B Complete the sentences.

1 My best friend is _____very tall_____. (height)
2 My best friend is _____. (looks)
3 My best friend has _____. (hair)
4 I am _____. (height)
5 I am _____. (looks)

Listen

Listen again. Then, complete the conversation.

Rick   I have a new girlfriend.
Minhee   That's great. What does she _____?
Rick   She's really pretty. And she has _____.
Minhee   Wow! _____ is she?
Rick   She's _____.
Minhee   I'd like to meet her sometime.

Your Turn to Speak

Talk to three other students. Ask them questions. Then, write the answers.

What does he/she look like?
How tall is he/she?
What hairstyle does he/she have?

	Student ❶	Student ❷	Student ❸
looks			
height			
hairstyle			

Conversation ❷ Body Shapes — Track 29

Listen carefully. Then, practice the following conversation with your partner.

Julie — I need to start working out.
Sungmin — Why do you think so?
Julie — I'm overweight. I want to be smaller.
Sungmin — You don't look overweight to me.
Julie — Thanks for saying that.

Focus

A Look at the pictures. Then, practice the expressions.

She is thin.
She is skinny.
She is slim.

He is average sized.

He has a good body.
He is in shape.
He is well built.

He is overweight.
He is out of shape.
He needs to lose weight.

She is underweight.
She needs to gain weight.

B Match the sentences.

1. Minhee needs to gain weight.
2. Rick is not too big and not too small.
3. Sungmin goes to the gym every day.
4. Mr. Jones is too fat.
5. Lisa never exercises.
6. Tom is too skinny.
7. The men love lifting weights.
8. Ms. Smith runs 2 hours every day.

ⓐ He needs to lose weight.
ⓑ She is underweight.
ⓒ He is in good shape.
ⓓ She is out of shape.
ⓔ He is average sized.
ⓕ They are well built.
ⓖ She has a good body.
ⓗ He is underweight.

C Describe the people in the pictures. What do they look like?

1 What kind of body does she have? _____
2 What kind of body does he have? _____
3 Is she in good or bad shape? _____
4 Is he in good or bad shape? _____
5 What kind of hair does she have? _____
6 What kind of hair does he have? _____

Listen

Listen again. Then, complete the conversation.

Julie   I need to start _____.
Sungmin   Why do you think so?
Julie   I'm _____. I want to be _____.
Sungmin   You don't _____ to me.
Julie   Thanks for saying that.

Your Turn to Speak

Talk to three other students. Ask them questions. Then, write the answers.

A What kind of <u>hair</u> do you have?
B I have long black hair.

	Student ❶	Student ❷	Student ❸
hair			
body			
eyes			

Conversation 3 — Clothes

Track 30

Listen carefully. Then, practice the following conversation with your partner.

Rick	Are we still going out tonight?
Minhee	Yes, we are.
Rick	Great. What are you wearing?
Minhee	I'm wearing black pants and a white blouse. How about you?
Rick	Hmm... I'm wearing a blue dress shirt and khaki pants.
Minhee	Okay. I'll see you later this evening.

Focus

A Look at the pictures. Then, practice the expressions.

T-shirt

polo shirt

button-down shirt
dress shirt

blouse

(blue) jeans

shorts

suit

skirt

dress

sweater

jacket

coat

84   English Communication 1

B Match the pictures and sentences.

ⓐ He's wearing a checkered shirt with long sleeves.
ⓑ She's wearing a flowered dress.
ⓒ He's wearing a suit.
ⓓ She's wearing a blouse and a skirt.
ⓔ He's wearing a T-shirt and blue jeans.

❶ ☐   ❷ ☐   ❸ ☐   ❹ ☐   ❺ ☐

C Write "casual" or "formal" next to the following descriptions.

1 I'm wearing blue jeans and a T-shirt.   _casual_
2 Jason is wearing shorts.   _____
3 Mijin is wearing a black dress.   _____
4 Minho is wearing a red shirt and light pants.   _____
5 They are wearing gray suits.   _formal_
6 Mr. Smith is wearing a black bowtie and a tuxedo.   _____
7 Miss Kim is wearing jeans, a green shirt, and sneakers.   _____
8 I'm wearing a white blouse, a skirt, and high heels.   _____

D Look at the pictures. What is each person wearing?

1 The man _____.
2 The woman _____.

Listen

Listen again. Then, complete the conversation.

Rick   Are we still _____ tonight?

Minhee   Yes, we are.

Rick   Great. What are you _____?

Minhee   I'm wearing black _____ and a white _____. How about you?

Rick   Hmm... I'm wearing a blue _____ and _____.

Minhee   Okay. I'll see you later this evening.

Your Turn to Speak

Talk to three other students. Ask them questions. Then, write the answers.

A What kind of shirt are you wearing?
B I'm wearing a green T-shirt.

	Student ❶	Student ❷	Student ❸
shirt			
shoes			
accessories			

Let's Practice Pronunciation

Track 31

Pronunciation

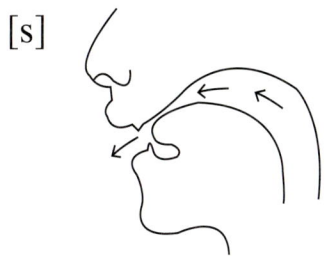
[s]

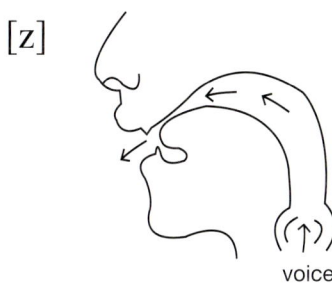
[z] voice

Word Comparison

[s] and [z] have different sounds. Try pronouncing the words below.

[s]	sap	sue	lace	seal	dose	bus	sip	fussy
[z]	zap	zoo	laze	zeal	doze	buzz	zip	fuzzy

Sentences

Read the following sentences. Try to pronounce [s] and [z] correctly.

1. **Excuse** me, **please**. I have a cold, **so** I am **sneezing**.
2. The **bees buzzed busily** around the **flowers**.
3. **Please use these slippers** in the **house**.
4. **Sam used** a **razor** to trim the hair on **his face**.
5. **Six cats chased** the **mouse** between the **trays**.

Sentence Patterns

1. She is _____.

   pretty | beautiful | average looking

   그녀는 _____ 하다.

   예쁜 | 아름다운 | 평범하게 생긴

2. She has _____.

   short hair | long, straight hair | curly brown hair

   그녀는 _____을 가지고 있다.

   짧은 머리 | 긴 생머리 | 갈색 곱슬머리

3. She's wearing _____.

   a white blouse and blue jeans

   a swimsuit

   a short-sleeved shirt and a blue striped skirt

   그녀는 _____을 입고 있다.

   흰 블라우스와 청바지

   수영복

   반팔 셔츠와 파란색 줄무늬 치마

Let's Read

Being Too Honest
Telling White Lies

Koreans are often very honest when they talk to other people. But sometimes Koreans can be TOO honest. You should be careful about speaking too directly to people. Here are some examples of being too honest:

> You look fat.
> You are ugly.
> That shirt looks terrible.

People always appreciate honesty, and nobody likes a liar. But sometimes you should not be totally honest. To avoid hurting people's feelings, don't always answer directly or honestly. Instead, give an answer that avoids answering the question. For example, if someone asks you what another person looks like, DON'T say, "She's ugly." That's not polite. Instead, use a different kind of answer:

> A: What does she look like?
> B: She's not my type. But maybe you'll like her.

You are not lying; you just aren't answering the question. Or, when talking about clothes, perhaps a person is wearing something that doesn't look good. Don't say, "That shirt is ugly," or, "You look fat in that shirt." Instead, say something like this:

> A: What do you think of my shirt?
> B: Um... maybe you should wear something else.

OR

> A: What do you think of my shirt?
> B: It's not my style.

Let's Talk More

1. Do you ever tell "white lies"? What kind of white lies do you tell?
2. When is it okay to tell a white lie?
3. Do you think you are too honest? Why or why not?

UNIT 09 I can do it.

Vocabulary

- ability 능력
- skill 기능, 기술, 솜씨
- bored 지루한
- nowadays 요즘
- try -ing ~을 시도하다
- musical instrument 악기
- excited 신난, 흥분한
- safe driver 안전 운전자
- take a ride (차를) 타다
- serious 진담의, 진지한, 심각한
- have to ~해야 한다
- must ~해야 한다
- should ~하는 게 좋다
- ought to ~하는 게 좋다

Get Ready

What can you do well? Check (✓) the skills and abilities. Then, talk to your partner.

Abilities and Skills (Talents)					
	Can	Cannot		Can	Cannot
snowboard			draw a picture		
fix a car			play the piano		
bake a cake			download an application		
play basketball			play the violin		
do yoga			jog for 20 minutes		
sing a song in English			design a webpage		
tell a good joke			ride a horse		

Conversation 1   Abilities with "Can"

Track 32

Listen carefully. Then, practice the following conversation with your partner.

Sungmin   I need a hobby. I'm bored nowadays.
Julie   You should try swimming. That's a lot of fun.
Sungmin   I can't swim.
Julie   Oh... can you play the piano?
Sungmin   No, I can't do that. I can't play any musical instruments.
Julie   Well, what can you do?

Focus

A Ask your partner questions. Write "can" or "cannot" beside each expression.

A   Can you use a computer?
B   Yes, I can. / No, I can't.

Can you _____?

- use a computer
- play a musical instrument
- paint a picture
- drive a car
- dance
- speak a foreign language
- swim
- cook
- play a sport
- skate

B Answer the questions about yourself.

1   Can you learn languages well?   _____
2   Can you play sports well?   _____
3   Can you sing well?   _____
4   Can you do your job well?   _____
5   Can you make friends easily?   _____
6   Can you do your homework easily?   _____

C *Think about your abilities. Write them in the boxes.*

Listen

Listen again. Then, complete the conversation.

Sungmin I need a _____. I'm _____ nowadays.

Julie You should try swimming. That's a lot of fun.

Sungmin I _____ swim.

Julie Oh... can you _____?

Sungmin No, I can't do that. I _____ any musical instruments.

Julie Well, What _____?

Conversation 2 — How Well You Can Do Something

Track 33

Listen carefully. Then, practice the following conversation with your partner.

Julie	I just bought a new car today. I'm so excited.
Tom	You can drive? I didn't know that.
Julie	Yes, I can drive. But I can't drive very well.
Tom	Are you a safe driver?
Julie	Of course. You can ride in my car with me now.
Tom	That's okay. Maybe later.

Focus

A Match the jobs with the abilities.

1. Minho is a programmer.
2. Sumi is a translator.
3. Tom is a doctor.
4. Sangmi is an architect.
5. Kevin is a pilot.
6. Brad is a clown.
7. Molly is an entertainer.
8. Miss Lee is a tour guide.

ⓐ She can take people on trips.
ⓑ He can use a computer well.
ⓒ She can sing and dance very well.
ⓓ He can help sick people.
ⓔ He can fly an aircraft.
ⓕ She is able to speak a foreign language.
ⓖ He can make people smile.
ⓗ She is able to design buildings.

B Answer the questions about yourself.

> A Can you cook well?
> B Yes, I can. I'm really good at it.

Positive Answer	Negative Answer
Yes, I can do it very well.	No, I can't do it at all.
Yes, I can do it a little.	No, I'm very bad at it.
I'm really good at it.	I don't know how to do it.

1   Can you cook well?   _____
2   Can you do your major well? _____
3   Can you dance well?   _____
4   Can you draw pictures well? _____
5   Can you speak English well? _____

C   *Look at the words. Then, make sentences with them. Use "can" or "can't."*

> a bird / sing   → A bird can sing.
> a horse / sing   → A horse can't sing.

A bird / fly
→ A bird _can fly_ .

a pig / fly
→ A pig _____ .

an elephant / climb a tree
→ An elephant _____ .

a boat / float on water
→ A boat _____ .

a baby / run fast
→ A baby _____ .

a child / read a book
→ A child _____ .

Listen

Listen again. Then, complete the conversation.

Julie   I just _____ a new car today. I'm so excited.

Tom   You can drive? I didn't know that.

Julie   Yes, I _____. But I can't drive _____.

Tom   Are you a _____?

Julie   Of course. You can _____ with me now.

Tom   That's okay. Maybe later.

Conversation 3 — Requirements and Obligations

Track 34

Listen carefully. Then, practice the following conversation with your partner.

Jihye	What time is it?
Rick	It's 10:00. Why?
Jihye	Are you serious? I have to go home now.
Rick	Really? You have to do that?
Jihye	Yes, I must. Or my mother will be very angry.
Rick	Oh... then you ought to go home right now.

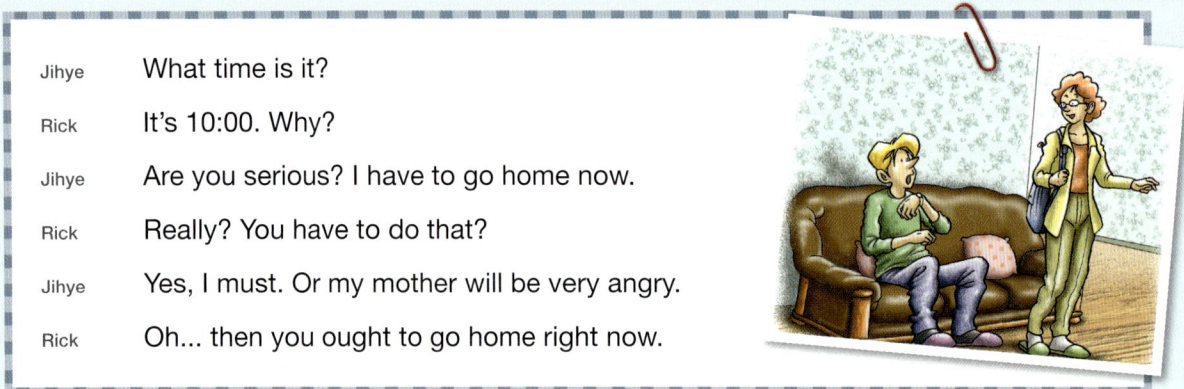

Focus

A Ask your partner questions. Then, write the answers.

> A What do you have to do in the morning?
> B I have to go to work in the morning.

What do you have to do _____?

- in the morning
- in the evening
- every day
- after work
- at home
- in the afternoon
- at night
- on the weekend
- after school
- before bed

B Answer the questions about yourself.

1. What do you have to do every day? <u>I have to work every day.</u>
2. What do you have to do in the morning? _____
3. What must you do in the evening? _____
4. What must you do after work? _____
5. Do you have to do your homework? _____
6. Where do you have to go after class? _____
7. Who must you meet this weekend? _____

C Look at the forms below. Then, complete the sentences.

> **have to, must, ought to, & should**
>
> **Have to**, **must**, **ought to**, and **should** have different meanings.
> **Have to** and **must** have the same meaning.
> **Have to** and **must** mean something is required.
> **Ought to** and **should** have the same meaning.
> **Ought to** and **should** mean something is a good idea, but it is not required.
>
> I have to go home. (→ I'm required to go home.)
> I must go home. (→ I'm required to go home.)
> I ought to go home. (→ I'm not required to go home, but it is a good idea.)
> I should go home. (→ I'm not required to go home, but it is a good idea.)

1 After class, I have to _____.
2 After class, I ought to _____.
3 Tomorrow morning, I must _____.
4 Tomorrow morning, I should _____.
5 Every day, I have to _____.
6 Every day, I ought to _____.
7 Next week, I have to _____.
8 Next week, I should _____.
9 Next vacation, I have to _____.
10 Next vacation, I ought to _____.
11 In the future, I must _____.
12 In the future, I should _____.

D Circle the mistakes. Then, write the correct sentences.

1 My sister (have) to go home soon.   My sister has to go home soon.
2 I can playing baseball very well.   _____
3 Miss Smith is able travel to many different places.   _____
4 William can no drive a bus.   _____
5 The teacher ought to coming to school early.   _____
6 She must calls me very soon.   _____

E *Write the correct words. Use the words in parentheses.*

1 I _____ (have to, should) do my homework, or I will get a zero.
2 Janet _____ (must, ought to) take a vacation soon. She looks tired.
3 Minho _____ (has to, ought to) exercise more often.
4 It's snowing! You _____ (must, should) wear a jacket, or you'll get sick.
5 She must go to work early. So she _____ (has to, should) wake up at 6 A.M.
6 We _____ (must, ought to) eat, or we won't have any energy.
7 You _____ (have to, should) ask Eungyoung out on a date.
8 I _____ (have to, ought to) go to sleep now. It's too late.

Listen

Listen again. Then, complete the conversation.

Jihye	What time is it?
Rick	It's 10:00. Why?
Jihye	Are you _____? I _____ go home now.
Rick	Really? You have to do that?
Jihye	Yes, I _____. Or my mother will be very angry.
Rick	Oh... then you _____ go home right now.

Your Turn to Speak

Talk to three other students. Ask them questions. Then, write the answers.

A What do you have to do today?
B I have to study for a test today.

	Student ❶	Student ❷	Student ❸
have to			
must			
ought to			
should			

Let's Practice Pronunciation

Track 35

Pronunciation

[t] 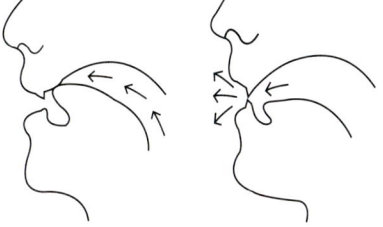   [d]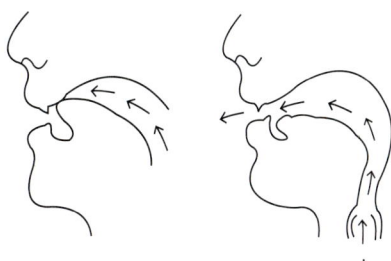

voice

Word Comparison

[t] and [d] have different sounds. Try pronouncing the words below.

[t]	tear	till	tent	tuck	right	catty	bat	seat	coat	time
[d]	dear	dill	dent	duck	ride	caddy	bad	seed	code	dime

Sentences

Read the following sentences. Try to pronounce [t] and [d] correctly.

1 They are **putting** some **pudding** in the bowls.
2 The **two lads went to** the **pond**.
3 **Tim rode right past** the **duck**.
4 I **bet** you will **stay** in **bed**.
5 The **fat lady ate too** much **food at** the **dinner party**.

Sentence Patterns

1 Can you _____?
   play the piano | draw | speak Chinese

   당신은 _____ 할 수 있어요?
   피아노를 치다 | 그림을 그리다 | 중국어를 말하다

2 I can't _____ very well.
   drive | play soccer | swim

   나는 _____ 을(를) 잘 못해요.
   운전하다 | 축구 하다 | 수영하다

3 I have to _____ now.
   go home | do my homework | meet my friend

   나는 지금 _____ 해야 합니다.
   집에 가다 | 숙제를 하다 | 친구를 만나다

Unit 09 I can do it. 97

Let's Read

Other Uses of "Can"
Giving Encouragement and Asking for Permission

We often use "can + verb" to talk about abilities, but we can also use it in a couple of other ways.

One way is to encourage people. For example, a person might not believe that he can do something successfully. To encourage this person, you could say, "You can do it!" or, "I know you can do it!" Americans often use these expressions to encourage people. In addition you can be more specific and say:

You can answer this question.
You can solve this problem.
You can win the game.

Another use of "can" is to ask for permission. If you want to do something, try asking:

Can I go out tonight?
Can I meet you later?
Can I borrow some money?

Of course, to be more polite, don't use "can." Instead, use "may." Like this:

May I go out tonight?
May I meet you later?
May I borrow some money?

In American culture, it's often better to use "may" instead of "can" when asking for permission. "May" is more polite. Still, many Americans often use "can" to ask for permission.

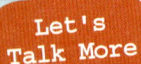

Let's Talk More

1. What do you say to encourage people?
2. What do you usually ask permission for?
3. Is it important to be polite when you ask for permission? Why?

UNIT 10 What did you do yesterday?

Vocabulary

- tired 피곤한
- stay up 밤새다
- all night long 밤새도록
- take a test 시험을 보다
- Good luck! 행운을 빌어!
- go to work 출근하다
- stay home 집에 있다
- all day long 하루 종일
- a while ago 조금 전에
- a long time ago 오래 전에
- the day before yesterday 그저께
- last 바로 요전의, 지난, 마지막의

Get Ready

Work with a partner. Ask and answer questions about your weekend.

A What did you do last weekend?
B I went to a movie.

What did you do last weekend?

- drink too much (= get drunk)
- play a video game
- do a homework assignment
- sleep
- clean the house
- go to a movie
- go on a date
- meet friends
- surf the Internet
- eat out
- stay home
- read a book

Conversation 1 — Past Activities

Track 36

Listen carefully. Then, practice the following conversation with your partner.

Sungmin You look tired today. Are you all right?

Jihye I stayed up all night long.

Sungmin Why did you do that?

Jihye I studied math last night. I am taking a test this afternoon.

Sungmin Oh. Good luck on the test.

Jihye Thanks.

Focus

A Look at these regular verbs. The past tense forms of these verbs end in -ed.

Regular Verbs in the Past Tense

Rule 1	rain	→	rained	Rule 4	study	→	studied
	ask	→	asked		carry	→	carried
Rule 2	smile	→	smiled	Rule 5	play	→	played
	erase	→	erased		enjoy	→	enjoyed
Rule 3	stop	→	stopped				
	rub	→	rubbed				

*The ending -ed has three pronunciations: [t], [d], and [id].

B Write the past tense forms of the following verbs.

1 clean _____
2 watch _____
3 climb _____
4 play _____
5 arrive _____
6 return _____
7 lie _____
8 study _____
9 stop _____
10 start _____
11 marry _____
12 love _____

C Work with a partner. Think about your last vacation. Make questions from the words. Then, ask and answer the questions with your partner.

1. Where / go?   Where did you go on your last vacation?
2. When / go?
3. Where / stay?
4. Who / go with?
5. How long / stay?
6. What / do?
7. Whom / meet?
8. What / buy?

Listen

Listen again. Then, complete the conversation.

Sungmin	You look _____ today. Are you all right?
Jihye	I _____ all night long.
Sungmin	Why did you do that?
Jihye	I _____ last night. I _____ a test this afternoon.
Sungmin	Oh. _____ on the test.
Jihye	Thanks.

Your Turn to Speak

Talk to three other students. Ask them questions. Then, write the answers.

A What did you do yesterday at 9:00 A.M.?
B I ate breakfast yesterday at 9:00 A.M.

	Student ❶	Student ❷	Student ❸
9:00 A.M.			
1:00 P.M.			
6:00 P.M.			
11:00 P.M.			

Conversation 2 — Times of Past Activities — Track 37

Listen carefully. Then, practice the following conversation with your partner.

Rick	What did you do yesterday?
Minhee	I went to work in the morning.
Rick	What time did you go to work?
Minhee	Around 9 A.M. Then, I met my friend at 7:00.
Rick	Oh. I watched a movie last night.
Minhee	I hope you had a good time.

Focus

A Look at these irregular verbs. The past tense forms these verbs do NOT end in -ed. They have different endings.

Irregular Verbs in the Past Tense

begin	→	began	bring	→	brought	come	→	came
do	→	did	drink	→	drank	eat	→	ate
get	→	got	give	→	gave	go	→	went
have	→	had	leave	→	left	make	→	made
read	→	read	see	→	saw	sleep	→	slept
think	→	thought	wake	→	woke	write	→	wrote

B Change the verbs to the past tense. Then, complete the sentences.

~~go~~	see	eat	put	write	sit	come

1. We ____went____ to the park last evening.
2. I _____ my teacher at the theater yesterday.
3. He _____ the milk in the refrigerator last night.
4. My husband _____ home around six this evening.
5. Eungyoung _____ lunch in the cafeteria three hours ago.
6. Mark _____ on the sofa and watched television.
7. I _____ a letter to my parents last month.

C Ask your partner questions. Then, write the answers.

> A   What did you do yesterday at <u>7:00</u> A.M.?
>
> B   I jogged.

What did you do yesterday at _____?

- 7:00 A.M.
- 9:00 A.M.
- 12:00 P.M.
- 3:00 P.M.
- 6:00 P.M.
- 10:00 P.M.

D Answer the questions.

1 What did you do yesterday at 7:00 A.M.?   <u>I woke up at 7:00 A.M. yesterday.</u>

2 What did you do yesterday at 12:00 P.M.?   _____

3 What did you do yesterday at 5:00 P.M.?   _____

4 What did you do yesterday at 8:00 P.M.?   _____

5 What did you do last weekend?   _____

6 What did you eat this morning?   _____

7 What did you watch on TV yesterday?   _____

Listen

Listen again. Then, complete the conversation.

Rick   What _____ you _____ yesterday?

Minhee I _____ to work in the morning.

Rick   What time did you go to work?

Minhee Around 9 A.M. Then, I _____ my friend at 7:00.

Rick   Oh. I _____ a movie last night.

Minhee I hope you _____ a good time.

Conversation 3 — Using Time Expressions in the Past

Track 38

Listen carefully. Then, practice the following conversation with your partner.

Julie	Did you have a good weekend?
Minho	Yes, I did. I saw a movie on Saturday.
Julie	Really? Who did you go with?
Minho	I went with my best friend Rick. What about you?
Julie	I stayed home and watched TV all day long.

Focus

A Look at the past time expressions and practice them.

- at 10:30 / around 10:00 A.M. / about 8:00 P.M.
- yesterday / the day before yesterday
- last night / last weekend / last week / last month / last year / last Friday / last spring / last winter
- five minutes ago / one hour ago / 2 days ago / 3 weeks ago
- a while ago / a long time ago

B Answer the questions.

1. What did you learn five minutes ago? _____
2. When did you wake up this morning? _____
3. Where did you have dinner last night? _____
4. Who did you meet yesterday? _____
5. What did you do two days ago? _____
6. Who did you call last weekend? _____
7. What did you study last week? _____
8. Where did you go last summer winter vacation? _____

C Complete the sentences. Use the past time words "ago," "yesterday," or "last."

1. I dreamed about you __last__ night.
2. My family moved into our new house _____ year.
3. I'm in Incheon today, but I was in Seoul _____.
4. 10 years _____, there weren't any houses in this area.
5. It rained _____.
6. We watched a movie _____ night.
7. I met my best friend 3 years _____.
8. Eric played with his children _____ evening.

D Match the questions with the answers.

1. Where did you go last weekend?
2. Who did Sara meet yesterday?
3. What did Julie eat last night?
4. How did you like the movie?
5. When did Jason leave work?
6. What did Mark do yesterday?
7. Where did Cindy go last summer?

ⓐ She took a trip to England.
ⓑ I went to Busan on Saturday.
ⓒ He watched TV with his friends.
ⓓ She had pizza for dinner.
ⓔ She met her friend last night.
ⓕ He left work at 6:00.
ⓖ It was great.

E Complete the sentences by using the past tense.

On Saturday night, I (1) _____ (wait) for a phone call, but my friend (2) _____ (not call). So I just (3) _____ (stay) home and (4) _____ (watch) television. On Sunday, I (5) _____ (visit) my sister. We (6) _____ (talk) and (7) _____ (listen) to some music. In the evening, she (8) _____ (invite) some friends over, and we (9) _____ (cook) a great meal. I (10) _____ (not work) very hard on the weekend. I (11) _____ (not study) at all.

F *Circle the mistakes. Then, write the correct answers.*

1. Who did you meet two ~~day~~ ago? _____ days _____
2. They ~~plaied~~ a game this morning. _____ played _____
3. They ~~last year moved~~ to a new home. _____ moved last year _____
4. I sleeped for eight hours last night. _____ slept _____
5. What did you ~~did~~ last weekend? _____ do _____
6. Mr. Smith called me ~~ago five minutes~~. _____ five minutes ago _____
7. I ate breakfast ~~in~~ 7:00 this morning. _____ at _____
8. We ~~bringed~~ our lunches to school yesterday. _____ brought _____

Listen

Listen again. Then, complete the conversation.

Julie Did you have a good weekend?

Minho Yes, I did. I _____ a movie on Saturday.

Julie Really? Who did you go with?

Minho I _____ with my best friend Rick. What about you?

Julie I _____ home and _____ TV all day long.

Your Turn to Speak

Talk to three other students. Ask them questions. Then, write the answers.

A: <u>What did you do</u> last weekend?
B: I went to the park last weekend.

	Student ❶	Student ❷	Student ❸
What did you do			
Who did you meet			
Where did you go			
What did you eat			

Let's Practice Pronunciation

Track 39

Pronunciation

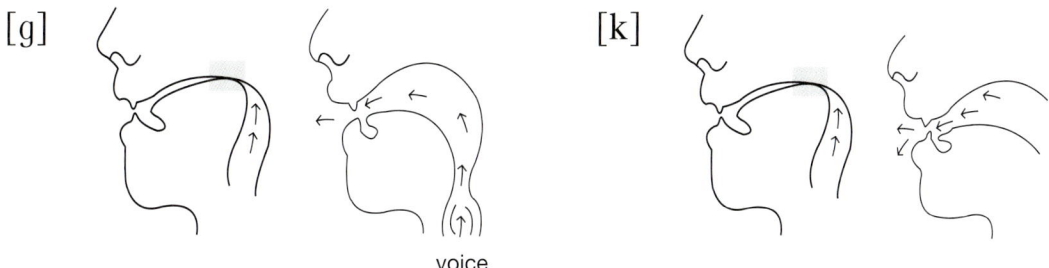

voice

Word Comparison

[g] and [k] have different sounds. Try pronouncing the words below.

| [g] | bag | game | gave | peg | log | angle | bagging | piggy | gum |
| [k] | back | came | cave | peck | lock | ankle | backing | picky | come |

Sentences

Read the following sentences. Try to pronounce [g] and [k] correctly.

1 The **soccer** player **scored** a **goal** during the **game**.
2 Who **came** to the **garden**?
3 **Kyle gave Glen** a **carpet** for his **kitchen**.
4 Would you **care** for a **snack**, **Kate**?
5 The **gang gathered together** at **Cape Park**.

Sentence Patterns

1 I _____ all night long.　　　　나는 밤새 _____ 했다.
   stayed up | studied | talked to my friend　　자지 않았다 | 공부했다 | 친구와 얘기했다

2 What did you do _____?　　　　당신은 _____ 무엇을 했습니까?
   yesterday | at 2:00 P.M. | last weekend　　어제 | 오후 2시에 | 지난 주에

3 Did you have _____?　　　　_____ 보냈나요?
   a good weekend | a good night | a good time　　좋은 주말 | 좋은 밤 | 좋은 시간

Unit 10 What did you do yesterday? 107

Let's Read

Nothing Special
Keeping Things Secret

Sometimes you might not feel like telling someone about what you did. Perhaps you don't feel like talking. Or perhaps you want to keep your actions a secret. Whatever the case, if you want to indicate that you don't want to give a detailed answer, try using the expression "Nothing special." For example, you might have a conversation like this:

A: What did you do last weekend?
B: Nothing special.

Americans use this expression all the time. When a person hears this, he will understand that you don't want to talk about that subject. He should then change the topic and talk about something different. So don't be rude and ask more questions to try to get more information.

Of course, you can also use this expression to talk about your future plans. Perhaps you are going on a date, but you don't want your friends to know about it. This is the perfect time to say, "Nothing special." Just like this:

A: What are you doing this evening?
B: Nothing special.

But be careful. When you use this expression, people might understand that you are trying to hide something. So if your friend is really nosy, he might keep asking you questions even if it is rather rude of him.

Let's Talk More

1. What do you do when you don't want to answer a question?
2. What are some situations when you can say, "Nothing special"?
3. Do you think you are a nosy person? Why or why not?

UNIT 11 I had long hair when I was young.

Vocabulary

- look at ~을 보다
- photo album 사진첩
- a picture of ~의 사진
- when I was young 내가 어렸을 때
- in the country 시골에
- have a good time 즐거운 시간을 보내다
- in high school 고등학교 시절에
- have fun 재미있다
- used to 예전에 ~했다
- Did you use to ~? 예전에 ~했나요?
- academy 학원
- talkative 수다스러운, 말이 많은

Get Ready

Work with a partner. Make questions with the expressions in the box.
Then, ask and answer the questions with your partner.

A　Did you go anywhere interesting last vacation?
B　Yes, I did. I went to Jeju Island with my family.

Did you _____ last vacation?

- go anywhere interesting
- have fun
- buy any souvenirs
- take any pictures
- eat any new foods
- have any interesting experiences

Conversation 1 — Talking about the Past — Track 40

Listen carefully. Then, practice the following conversation with your partner.

Minhee	What are you looking at?
Jihye	This is a photo album. I'm looking at some old pictures.
Minhee	Hey! Is that a picture of you?
Jihye	Yes. I had long hair when I was young.
Minhee	When you were young, did you live in Seoul?
Jihye	No. I lived in the country.

Focus

A Match the question words with the correct phrases.

1. What?
2. How many?
3. Who?
4. What time?
5. Why?
6. Where?
7. How much?
8. When?

ⓐ At the park.
ⓑ 9:30 P.M.
ⓒ A dog.
ⓓ Twelve.
ⓔ Billy.
ⓕ Because he is young.
ⓖ On Thursday.
ⓗ Two dollars.

B Ask your partner questions. Then, write the answers.

A	When you were young, did you like school?
B	No. I sometimes cut classes.

When you were young, _____?

- did you like school
- did you have a pet
- did you ride a bicycle
- did you play outside
- what sports did you play
- where did you live
- what books did you read
- who was your best friend

110   English Communication 1

C *Answer the questions about yourself.*

1   When you were young, did you like school? _____
2   When you were young, did you have a pet? _____
3   When you were young, did you learn English? _____
4   When you were young, did you play sports? _____
5   When you were young, what was your hobby? _____
6   When you were young, where did you live? _____
7   When you were young, who was your best friend? _____
8   When you were young, what did you do after school? _____

D *Look at the answers. Make questions with wh-question words.*

A	What time did you finish your homework?
B	I finished my homework **around six o'clock**.

1   A _____
    B I studied **math** after lunch.
2   A _____
    B I did not go to class **because** I was sick.
3   A _____
    B The baseball game began **at 8:30**.
4   A _____
    B My wife went to **the supermarket**.
5   A _____
    B I met him **two months ago**.

Listen

Listen again. Then, complete the conversation.

Minhee   What are you looking at?
Jihye   This is a photo album. I'm looking at some _____.
Minhee   Hey! Is that _____ you?
Jihye   Yes. I had long hair when I was _____.
Minhee   When you _____ young, _____ in Seoul?
Jihye   No. I _____ in the country.

Conversation 2 — Past Activities   Track 41

Listen carefully. Then, practice the following conversation with your partner.

Rick	Did you have a good time in high school?
Sumi	Yeah. When I was in high school, I had fun.
Rick	Really? What did you do?
Sumi	I always played sports after school.
Rick	When you were a high school student, did you study hard?
Sumi	Sometimes. But I didn't study hard very often.

Focus

A *Answer "true" or "false."*

1. When I was a child, I was often happy. _____
2. When I was in elementary school, I had a pet dog. _____
3. When I was a middle school student, I lived in Seoul. _____
4. When I was a high school student, I always studied hard. _____
5. When I was fifteen years old, I had a boyfriend/girlfriend. _____
6. When I was eighteen years old, I used a social media site. _____

B *Complete the sentences.*

1. When I was young, I always listened to my parents. _____
2. When I was young, I never _____.
3. When I was young, my hobby was _____.
4. When I was young, my best friend _____.
5. When I was a high school student, I _____.
6. When I was a high school student, my parents _____.
7. When I was a high school student, my teachers _____.
8. When I was a high school student, school _____.

C   Work with a partner. Ask your partner the questions. Then, ask one more follow-up question.

> A   When was the last time you went to a movie?
> B   I went to a movie last weekend.
> A   Who did you go with?
> B   I went with my family.

When was the last time you _____?

- went to a movie   _last weekend / with her family_
- went on a date   _____
- got sick   _____
- sent a text message   _____
- helped someone   _____
- received a gift   _____

Listen

Listen again. Then, complete the conversation.

Rick	_____ you _____ in high school?
Sumi	Yeah. When I was in high school, I _____.
Rick	Really? What did you do?
Sumi	I always _____ after school.
Rick	When you were a high school student, did you study hard?
Sumi	Sometimes. But I didn't study hard _____.

Your Turn to Speak

Talk to three other students. Ask them questions. Then, write the answers.

"When you were young, _____?"

	Student ❶	Student ❷	Student ❸
were you a good boy/girl			
were you quiet or loud			
where did you live			

Unit 11   I had long hair when I was young.

Conversation 3 — Used To 🔘 Track 42

Listen carefully. Then, practice the following conversation with your partner.

Jack	Can you speak Chinese?
Minhee	I used to speak Chinese. But I don't anymore.
Jack	Me too. I learned it in high school.
Minhee	Did you use to go to an academy?
Jack	No, I never went to an academy.
Minhee	Oh. I used to go every day.

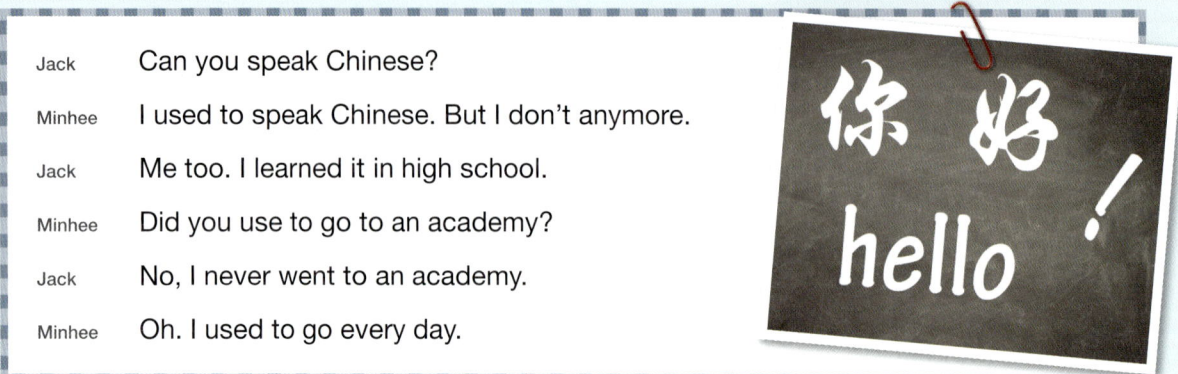

Focus

A Look at the form below and practice it.

> **used to + verb**
>
> Say **used to** when you talk about something you did in the past but do NOT do now. Do NOT use **used to** to talk about something you did in the past AND still do today. For **used to**, the past and present actions or activitiest must be different.
>
> I **used to** exercise every day, but now I don't.
> Sumi **used to** go to university, but now she has a job.
> Rick **used to** live in Japan, but now he lives in Korea.
> They **used to** play video games, but now they play computer games.
> We **used to** be bad students, but now we study hard.
> I **used to** be shy, but now I'm talkative.

B Ask your partner questions. Then, write the answers.

> **Did you use to _____?**
>
> ▫ read a lot   ▫ play video games
> ▫ have a pet   ▫ go to the countryside

What did you _____ **?**	
▫ always use to do	▫ often use to do
▫ sometimes use to do	▫ never use to do

C *Answer the questions about yourself.*

1. Where did you use to live when you were young?
   <u>I used to live in the country when I was young.</u>

2. Where did you use to play after school when you were young?
   _____

3. What did you use to do during summer vacation when you were in elementary school?
   _____

4. Who used to be your best friend when you were twelve years old?
   _____

5. Who used to be your favorite singer when you were in high school?
   _____

D *Match the questions and answers.*

1. Did you use to have a pet?
2. Did you use to read a lot?
3. What did you always use to do?
4. What did you never use to do?
5. Where did you use to live?
6. Who used to be your best friend?
7. Did you use to be talkative?
8. Did you use to have a hobby?

ⓐ I never used to surf the Internet.
ⓑ I used to live in Daegu.
ⓒ Yes. I used to do cross-stitching.
ⓓ No. But now I like reading books.
ⓔ Her name was Eunyoung.
ⓕ No. I used to be very shy.
ⓖ Yes. My dog's name was Friday.
ⓗ I always used to play with my friends.

E *Circle the mistakes. Then, write the correct sentences.*

1. Where did Jason used to live? _____
2. Kyoungmi used to working in a hospital. _____
3. Trevor used read books every day. _____
4. What are you use to play as a child? _____
5. He used to bad, but now he is nice. _____
6. Did use you to play the piano? _____

F   Complete the sentences. Use the words in the box.

play	be	like	cook	study	ride

Sungmin is twenty-two years old. When he was twelve years old, he was very different. He used to (1) _____ fat, but now he exercises every day. Sungmin always studies hard these days, but he never used to (2) _____ when he was young. He loves to drive his car now, but he used to (3) _____ his bicycle as a child. He plays soccer nowadays, but he used to (4) _____ basketball. He never used to (5) _____, but now he makes dinner for his girlfriend all the time. He meets his girlfriend every day. But when he was young, he didn't use to (6) _____ girls.

Listen

Listen again. Then, complete the conversation.

Jack   Can you speak Chinese?

Minhee   I _____ speak Chinese. But I don't anymore.

Jack   Me too. I _____ in high school.

Minhee   _____ you _____ go to an academy?

Jack   No, I never went to an academy.

Minhee   Oh. I _____ every day.

Your Turn to Speak

Talk to three other students. Ask them questions. Then, write the answers.

A Did you use to <u>have a hobby</u>?
B Yes, I did. I used to collect stamps.

	Student ❶	Student ❷	Student ❸
have a hobby			
study hard			
have short hair			

Let's Practice Pronunciation

Track 43

Pronunciation

[l]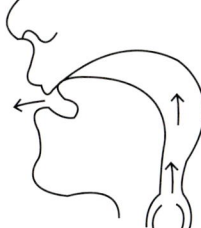

[r]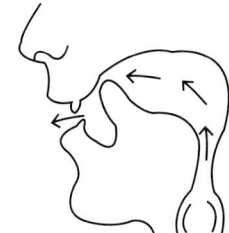

Word Comparison

[l] and [r] have different sounds. Try pronouncing the words below.

[l]	led	light	lice	gland	lock	link	play	elect	lobe	fly
[r]	red	right	rice	grand	rock	rink	pray	erect	robe	fry

Sentences

Read the following sentences. Try to pronounce [l] and [r] correctly.

1 The **rabbit raced around** the **large tree**.
2 The **crowd looked** at the **large ladder**.
3 The **little lamb ran happily** in the **field**.
4 He **threw** the **liver** into the **river**.
5 The **wrinkled old** woman **loves writing letters**.

Sentence Patterns

1 I had long hair when _____.

   I was young | I was in elementary school | I was sixteen

   _____ 일 때 머리가 길었어요.

   어렸을 때 | 초등학생 때 | 16살 때

2 When you were a high school student,
   did you _____?

   study hard | enjoy your classes | have a pet

   고등학생일 때 _____ 했나요?

   열심히 공부하다 | 수업을 즐기다 | 애완동물이 있다

3 I used to _____.

   go to the gym | watch TV every day | have many friends

   (예전에) 나는 _____ 하곤 했다.

   체육관에 다니다 | 매일 TV를 보다 | 친구가 많다

Let's Read

Talking to Foreigners

Starting a Conversation with a Foreigner

Sometimes you might see a foreigner and want to speak with that person. However, you might not know how to start the conversation. You might think, "What should I say?" There are many good expressions to use, but there are also some expressions that you should NOT use. For example, DON'T use the following expressions:

> Welcome to Korea.
> May I practice speaking English with you?
> How do you like Korea?

For most foreigners, these are bad conversation starters. If you say one of these expressions, the person will probably not want to talk to you.

Americans often start conversations with strangers by talking about unimportant things, such as the weather or sports. They also might talk about where they are going or what they are doing. Some good conversation starters are:

> Nice weather, isn't it?
> Where are you going?
> What brought you to Korea?

If the person just answers with a simple "Yes" or "No," then he probably doesn't want to talk. However, if he gives you a longer answer, you should be able to have a conversation. When that happens, good luck speaking English.

Let's Talk More

1. What are some bad conversation-starters?
2. What are some good conversation-starters?
3. Do you ever start conversations with strangers? What do you talk about?

UNIT 12 How about going out tonight?

Vocabulary

- Let's ~ 우리 ~하자
- We should ~ 우리 ~하자
- forget to ~ ~하는 것을 잊다
- How about -ing? ~하는 게 어때?
- go on a date 데이트 하다
- I'd love to! 좋아!
- May I speak to Tim? 팀 좀 바꿔 주시겠어요?
- Is Steve there? 스티브 있어요?
- He/She is not here right now. 지금 여기 없는데요.
- This is he/she. 전데요.
- Hold on, please. 잠깐만요.
  (= Just a minute, please.)
- May I take a message? 메시지 남겨드릴까요?
- Would you like to leave a message?
  메시지 남기시겠어요?
- Please tell her to call Julie.
  줄리에게 전화해 달라고 전해 주세요.

Get Ready

Look at the pictures of common places for dates. Then, talk to your partner.

1. Where do you usually go on a date?
2. Where is your favorite place to go on a date?
3. Where is your least favorite place to go on a date?

restaurant

park

café

your home

Conversation 1 Using "Let's" — Track 44

Listen carefully. Then, practice the following conversation with your partner.

Jack   I'm hungry. I forgot to have lunch today.
Minhee   Hmm... Let's go to dinner now.
Jack   Good idea. Where should we go?
Minhee   That's a good question.
Jack   I got it! Let's go to the new Italian restaurant.
Minhee   Yeah. We should have dinner there.

Focus

A *Complete the sentences with the verbs in the box.*

watch	buy	study	go	talk	do	clean

1 Let's __watch__ that new television program.
2 Let's _____ together at the library.
3 Let's _____ a trip to the East Sea this weekend.
4 Let's _____ shopping at the new department store.
5 We should _____ our homework every day.
6 We should _____ the car. It's too dirty.
7 Your girlfriend is angry with you.
   You should _____ her some flowers.

> **Let's + verb**
>
> ☐ Say **let's** when you make a suggestion.
> ☐ Use **let's** when you want to do something.

B *Complete the sentences with the expressions in the box.*

| leave at eight-thirty | go to Hawaii | eat | go to a concert |

1. A I'm bored. _____
   B I can't. I have to go to my part-time job.
   A That's too bad.
2. A Breakfast is ready. The dishes are on the table.
   B Great! I'm hungry. _____
3. A What time should we leave for the picnic?
   B _____
4. A Where should we go for our honeymoon?
   B _____
   A Okay. I'd love to go there.

C *Make suggestions for each problem.*

	Problems		Suggestions
1	I'm really hungry right now.	Let's	get something to eat.
2	We need some new clothes.	Let's	_____ .
3	We have a test tomorrow.	Let's	_____ .
4	This house is very dirty.	Let's	_____ .
5	It's really late right now.	We should	_____ .
6	That new movie starts tonight.	We should	_____ .
7	I have an interview tomorrow.	You should	_____ .
8	I'm so sleepy right now.	You should	_____ .

Listen

Listen again. Then, complete the conversation.

Jack I'm hungry. I forgot to have lunch today.

Minhee Hmm... _____ to dinner now.

Jack Good idea. Where _____?

Minhee That's a good question.

Jack I got it! Let's go to the new Italian restaurant.

Minhee Yeah. We _____ dinner there.

Conversation ❷ Making Invitations — Track 45

Listen carefully. Then, practice the following conversation with your partner.

Rick	Hello, Julie. How are you doing?
Julie	I'm great.
Rick	Are you busy tonight?
Julie	No, not really. Why do you ask?
Rick	How about going on a date with me?
Julie	I'd love to!

Focus

A *Practice the different ways to accept and reject invitations.*

Acceptance

- Okay. / Sure.
- That's a good idea.
- I'd like that. / I'd like to go out with you.
- I'd love to. / I'd love to see a movie with you.
- That sounds good (to me). / That sounds great (to me). / That sounds perfect (to me).

Rejection

- No thanks.
- Maybe another time.
- I already have plans.
- Sorry. I can't. / Sorry. I can't see a movie with you.
- I'd love to, but I'm busy. / I'd love to, but I have no time.

B *Accept or reject the invitations.*

1. How about going to a movie with me?   I'd love to. / Sorry. I can't.
2. How about having dinner with me?   _____
3. How about taking a walk with me?   _____
4. How about going out with me?   _____
5. Will you have a drink with me?   _____
6. Will you come to my party?   _____
7. Would you like to take a trip with me?   _____
8. Would you like to study with me?   _____

C Circle the incorrect parts. Then, write the correct sentences.

1 Let's (going) to the party.   Let's go to the party.
2 How about watch a movie with me? _____
3 What should we doing tonight? _____
4 Let's together have dinner. _____
5 I'd loved to go to the park with you. _____
6 Would you like meet me later tonight? _____

Listen

Listen again. Then, complete the conversation.

Rick   Hello, Julie. _____ are you doing?
Julie I'm _____.
Rick   Are you busy tonight?
Julie No, not really. Why do you ask?
Rick   _____ on a date with me?
Julie _____ love to!

Your Turn to Speak

Talk to three other students. Ask them questions. Then, write the answers.

A How about seeing a movie?
B That's a good idea.

	Student ❶	Student ❷	Student ❸
seeing a movie			
having dinner			
going shopping			
going to the park			

Conversation ❸ Talking on the Telephone — Track 46

Listen carefully. Then, practice the following conversation with your partner.

Jihye	Hello?
Sungmin	Hello. May I speak to Minhee, please?
Jihye	Sorry. She's not here right now.
Sungmin	Oh. That's too bad.
Jihye	May I take a message?
Sungmin	Yes. Please tell her to call Sungmin.

Focus

A *Practice these telephone expressions.*

Greetings	▫ Hello. May I speak to Jihye?	▫ Hello. Can I speak with Rick?
	▫ Hello. Is Sungmin there?	▫ Hello. Is Minhee available?
Answers	▫ This is he/she.	▫ This is Rick.
	▫ Just a minute, please.	▫ Hold on, please.
	▫ Sorry. He/She isn't here now.	▫ Sorry. Minhee is busy right now.
Messages	▫ May I take a message?	▫ Would you like to leave a message?
	▫ Can I leave a message?	▫ Will you take a message for me?
	▫ Tell Jihye to call Sungmin.	▫ Please ask Rick to call Julie.
	▫ Tell Minhee I'll call her later.	▫ Please tell Julie to meet me tonight.

B *Match the questions with the answers.*

1. May I speak to Kevin?
2. May I take a message?
3. Can I leave a message?
4. Can I speak to Jihye?
5. Hello. Is Minhee around?

ⓐ Just a moment, please.
ⓑ This is he.
ⓒ This is Jihye.
ⓓ Yes. Tell Julie to call me.
ⓔ Sure. What is it?

C Look at the example. Then, write similar questions and answers using the words in parentheses.

A	(speak, John)	Hello. May I speak to John?
B	(yes, minute)	Yes. Just a minute, please.

1 (Sangmi, there) _____
   (no, not here)   _____

2 (Mr. Lee, available) _____
   (yes, hold on)   _____

3 (Lisa, speak)   _____
   (no, busy)   _____

4 (Amy, there)   _____
   (yes, minute)   _____

D Complete the conversation.

sure	bye	may	message	sorry	give	ask

A Hello?

B Hello. (1) _____ I speak to Brian?

A (2) _____. He's not here right now.

B Really? Can I leave a (3) _____?

A (4) _____. What is it?

B Please (5) _____ Brian to call David tonight.

A Okay. I will (6) _____ him the message.

B Thanks. Bye.

A (7) _____.

E Leave messages for different people.

1 A Hello. May I speak to Sumi?

   B Sorry. She's not here. May I take a message?

   A Yes. Tell her _to call Lisa_ .

2 A Hi. Is Jason there?

   B He's busy right now. Would you like to leave a message?

   A Yes, I would. Please ask Jason _____.

Unit 12 How about going out tonight? 125

3 A Hello. Is Eungyoung available?

   B No, she's not. But I can take a message.

   A Okay. _____.

4 A Hi. Can I speak with Trevor?

   B I'm afraid he's not home now. Do you want to leave a message?

   A Sure. _____.

Listen

Listen again. Then, complete the conversation

Jihye	Hello?
Sungmin	Hello. May I _____ Minhee, please?
Jihye	Sorry. She's _____ right now.
Sungmin	Oh. That's too bad.
Jihye	_____ I take a _____?
Sungmin	Yes. _____ her to _____ Sungmin.

Your Turn to Speak

Talk to three other students. Ask them questions. Then, write the answers.

A Hello. May I speak to your <u>father</u>?

B Sorry. He's not here now.

	Student ❶	Student ❷	Student ❸
father			
mother			
sister			
brother			

Let's Practice Pronunciation — Track 47

Pronunciation

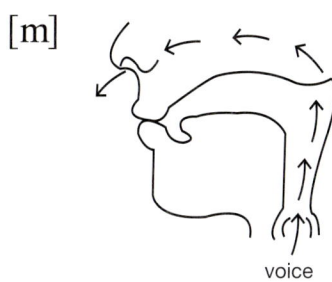
[m]
voice

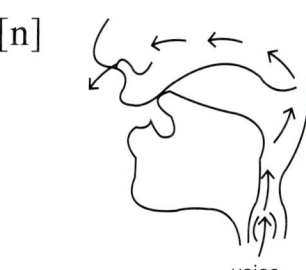
[n]
voice

Word Comparison

[m] and [n] have different sounds. Try pronouncing the words below.

[m]	seem	team	theme	ram	clam	mode	smack	dumb	simmer	meet
[n]	seen	thin	teen	ran	clan	node	snack	done	sinner	need

Sentences

Read the following sentences. Try to pronounce [m] and [n] correctly.

1. The **man nodded** to **Mark** in the **market**.
2. That **naughty monkey** bit the nice **man**.
3. Please invite **Matt** and **Nancy** to the **game** on Saturday.
4. The teen just **joined** the **team**.
5. How long was **Mary** in the **sun**?

Sentence Patterns

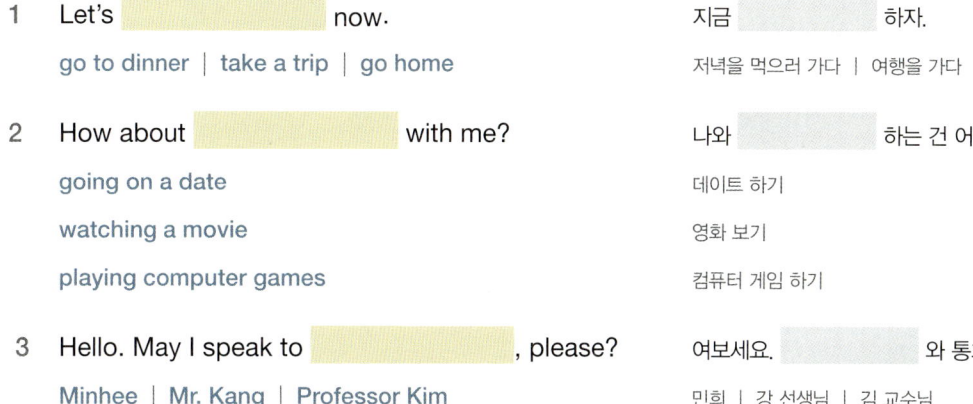

Unit **12** How about going out tonight?

Let's Read

Asking People out on Dates
Making Invitations

When you ask a person out on a date, it's better to use formal rather than casual language. For example, you should ask:

> How about going on a date with me?
> Would you like to see a movie with me?

These are formal expressions. And they are perfect for asking a person out on a date.

However, if you are just talking to your friend and making an invitation, you can use more casual language. You can say:

> Let's have dinner.
> We should go see a movie.

Of course, don't use "let's" or "we should" if you are asking a person out on a date. It's too informal, and the person might not think that you are very serious about going on a date. The person is likely to say no if you use casual language.

Additionally, in American culture, women often ask men out on dates. (Men like this a lot!) Traditionally, men ask women out on dates, but, nowadays if a woman likes a man, she may ask him out on a date. So, if you're a man, don't be surprised if a woman ever asks you out.

Let's Talk More

1. Where do you like to go on dates?
2. What are some good ways to ask a person out on a date?
3. Should women ask men out on dates? What do you think?

UNIT 13 I want to see a movie.

Vocabulary

- What do you want to do? 무엇을 하고 싶으세요?
- I want to ~ 난 ~하고 싶다
- something different 무언가 다른
- bar 바, 술집
- Would you like to ~? ~할래요?
- That's a great idea. 정말 좋은 생각이야.
- I'm starving. 배고파 죽겠어.
- That's fine with me. 저는 좋아요.
- I don't want to ~ ~하고 싶지 않다
- I'd like to ~ 난 ~하고 싶다
- How about ~? ~은 어때?

Get Ready

You're on vacation for one week. What do you want to do this week? Write your weekly schedule.

Monday	Tuesday	Wednesday	Thursday
go to the beach in the morning			

Friday	Saturday	Sunday

Conversation 1 Wants

Track 48

Listen carefully. Then, practice the following conversation with your partner.

Rick	I'm bored. Let's do something.
Sungmin	Okay. What do you want to do?
Rick	I want to see a movie.
Sungmin	Movies are boring. Let's do something different.
Rick	Well... do you want to go to a bar?
Sungmin	Great idea. Let's go.

Focus

A Ask your partner questions. Then, write the answers.

A	What do you want to do <u>today</u>?
B	I want to see a movie.

What do you want to do _____?

- today
- after work
- tomorrow morning
- this weekend
- next vacation
- tonight
- after school
- tomorrow evening
- next week
- next year

B Answer the questions about yourself.

1 What do you want to do today? _____

2 What do you want to do after school? _____

3 What do you want to do tomorrow? _____

4 What do you want to do this weekend? _____

5 Where do you want to go tonight? _____

6 What do you want to eat this evening? _____

C Complete the invitations with the words in the box. Then, match the invitations with the responses.

| walk | attend | go | ~~visit~~ | see | play | eat | study |

Invitation

1. Do you want to __visit__ Seoul Land this Sunday?
2. Do you want to _____ a concert tomorrow night?
3. Do you want to _____ to an art gallery this week?
4. Do you want to _____ basketball after work?
5. Do you want to _____ a movie with me this weekend?
6. Do you want to _____ my dog with me?
7. Do you want to _____ dinner at my house?
8. Do you want to _____ math together?

Response

ⓐ I don't really like basketball. Do you want to do something else?
ⓑ Tomorrow night? I'm sorry. I need to help my parents.
ⓒ I want to, but I can't. I am going on a trip this Sunday.
ⓓ Sure. I really want to see a good comedy.
ⓔ Yes, I want to go.
ⓕ Yes. I have some questions about it.
ⓖ Okay. I love animals.
ⓗ h. Sorry, but I'm not hungry now.

Listen

Listen again. Then, complete the conversation.

Rick I'm _____. Let's _____ something.
Sungmin Okay. What do you _____?
Rick I _____ see a movie.
Sungmin Movies are boring. Let's do something _____.
Rick Well... do you want to go to a bar?
Sungmin Great idea. Let's go.

Conversation ❷ Using "Would Like" ⊙ Track 49

Listen carefully. Then, practice the following conversation with your partner.

Greg	Would you like to have dinner?
Minhee	Sure. I'm starving.
Greg	Where would you like to eat?
Minhee	Anywhere is fine with me.
Greg	How about a Chinese restaurant?
Minhee	Okay. I know a great place. We can go there.

Focus

A Match the locations with the desires.

1. movie theater
2. department store
3. airport
4. music store
5. bus station
6. jewelry store
7. library
8. coffee shop

ⓐ William wants to fly to Japan.
ⓑ We want to take a trip to the countryside.
ⓒ Jinhee wants to talk to her friends.
ⓓ They would like to see a film.
ⓔ I'd like to buy some new CDs.
ⓕ The students would like to study.
ⓖ Sumi wants to buy some new clothes.
ⓗ Sangmi would like to purchase some gold earrings.

B Circle the incorrect parts. Then, write the correct sentences.

1. I want to ⊙going⊙ home now.   I want to go home now.
2. Mr. Kim would likes to meet Sumi.   _____
3. Julie would like watch that movie.   _____
4. Chris and Peter wants to learn how to drive.   _____
5. The dog wants eat that bone.   _____
6. What would like you to do?   _____
7. Where are you want to go?   _____
8. Would you liking to stay for dinner?   _____

132   English Communication 1

C *Complete the sentences.*

1 I want to _____see a movie_____ today.
2 I would like to _____ today.
3 I want to _____ every day.
4 I would like to _____ every day.
5 I want to _____ this weekend.
6 I would like to _____ this weekend.
7 What do you want to _____ tonight?
8 What would you like to _____ tonight?

Listen

Listen again. Then, complete the conversation.

Greg   _____ you _____ have dinner?
Minhee Sure. I'm _____.
Greg   _____ would you like to eat?
Minhee Anywhere is fine _____ me.
Greg   How about a Chinese restaurant?
Minhee Okay. I know a great _____. We can go there.

Your Turn to Speak

Talk to three other students. Ask them questions. Then, write the answers.

A What would you like to eat?
B I'd like to eat pizza.

	Student ❶	Student ❷	Student ❸
eat			
read			
buy			

Conversation 3 — Using "Don't Want"

Track 50

Listen carefully. Then, practice the following conversation with your partner.

Sumi   Let's do our homework.
Tom   No. I don't want to do homework now.
Sumi   Um... why not?
Tom   I don't know. I just don't want to do it.
Sumi   Okay. How about watching TV?
Tom   That's a great idea. I'd like to watch some TV now.

Focus

A Ask your partner questions. Then, write the answers.

What _____ do you not want to _____ ?

- song / listen to
- clothes / buy
- subject / study
- person / meet

What _____ would you not like to _____ ?

- computer game / play
- book / read
- meal / eat
- movie / see

B Answer the questions about yourself.

1. What song do you not want to listen to? <u>I don't want to listen to a pop song.</u>
2. What person do you not want to meet? _____
3. What food would you not like to cook? _____
4. What TV show would you not like to watch? _____
5. What country do you not want to visit? _____
6. What job would you not like to have? _____
7. Who do you not want to date? _____
8. Where would you not like to live? _____

134   English Communication 1

C   Read the suggestions. Give negative answers by using "want."

1   Let's do our homework now.   I don't want to do homework now.
2   Let's watch a movie tonight.   _____
3   Let's take a trip to China this summer. _____
4   We should go to the library tomorrow. _____
5   We should skip class tonight.   _____
6   We should cook dinner this evening.   _____

D   Match the reasons with the negative sentences.

1   Lewis doesn't want to play basketball.   ⓐ He likes to eat at restaurants.
2   Junga doesn't like to drive.   ⓑ She wants to see a movie.
3   Sangmi doesn't want to watch TV.   ⓒ He prefers country music.
4   Todd doesn't want to listen to dance music.   ⓓ He doesn't like sports.
5   Minsu doesn't like to cook.   ⓔ She is not a good student.
6   Cindy doesn't like to study.   ⓕ She's not a good driver.

E   Look at the form below and practice it.

> **because**
>
> Say **because** to answer the question "why." Use **because** to combine two sentences.
> **Because** should always give a reason.
>
> I like school **because** it is interesting.
> She wants to eat **because** she is hungry.
> He plays computer games **because** he enjoys them.
> I don't like spicy food **because** it is too hot.
> She doesn't want to study **because** she wants to play a game.
> He doesn't drive **because** he doesn't have a car.

F   Complete the sentences.

1   I like Korean food because ___it is delicious.___
2   Eungyoung likes her job because _____.
3   Rick listens to rock music because _____.
4   I don't watch horror movies because _____.
5   She doesn't read books because _____.
6   He doesn't wake up early because _____.

Listen

Listen again. Then, complete the conversation.

Sumi　　Let's do our homework.

Tom　　No. _____ to do homework now.

Sumi　　Um... _____ ?

Tom　　I don't know. I just don't want to do it.

Sumi　　Okay. How about _____ TV?

Tom　　That's a great idea. I'd like to _____ some TV now.

Your Turn to Speak

Talk to three other students. Ask them questions. Then, write the answers.

A What *do* you not want to *do*?
B I don't want to study math.

	Student ❶	Student ❷	Student ❸
do			
eat			
study			
buy			

Let's Practice Pronunciation

Track 51

Pronunciation

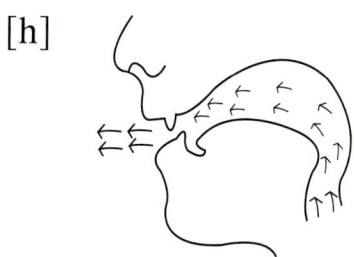

[h]

Word Comparison

Try pronouncing the words below.

[h]	have	hall	happy	hare	how	head	hay	hoot
	behind	behave	headquarters	hospital	hill	hedge	hold	bellhop

Sentences

Read the following sentences. Try to pronounce [h] correctly.

1 **He** did a lot of **harm** to the farm.
2 **Hey! How** can my **head** and **heart hurt** at the same time?
3 The **hospital's headquarters** are **behind** the **health** shop.
4 The **handsome hitchhiker hummed happily**.
5 **Hazel helped Harry hang** the **holly**.

Sentence Patterns

1 I want to _____.
   see a movie | use the computer | go shopping

   나는 _____ 하고 싶다.
   영화를 보다 | 컴퓨터를 사용하다 | 쇼핑하러 가다

2 Would you like to _____?
   have dinner | be my friend | wear this dress

   _____ 하실래요?
   저녁을 먹다 | 내 친구가 되다 | 이 드레스를 입다

3 I don't want to _____ now.
   do my homework | eat breakfast | leave home

   나는 지금 _____ 하고 싶지 않다.
   숙제를 하다 | 아침을 먹다 | 집을 떠나다

Unit 13 I want to see a movie.

Let's Read

Making Plans
Talking about What You Want to Do

One of the most common questions that people ask others is "What do you want to do?" This is especially common when people are making plans for the evening or weekend. In fact, you've probably done this many times!

When someone asks, "What do you want to do?" and you don't really care, you use these expressions:

>Anything.
>Anything is okay.
>It's up to you.

All of these expressions mean that you have no preference so you want the other person to decide. Another possible answer to the question is to say, "I don't know. What do you want to do?"

Of course, if the question changes slightly, your answer might have to change slightly. For example, to answer the question, "Where do you want to go?" you might say:

>Anywhere.
>Anywhere is fine.
>I don't care where we go.

These are just a few of the many answers that you can give.

Let's Talk More

1. How do you feel when someone answers "Anything"?
2. When you meet your friends, who decides where you will go?
3. Do you sometimes go to places with your friends, but you don't want to be there?

UNIT 14 What's the matter?

Vocabulary

- What's the matter? 무슨 일이죠?
- Oh, my gosh! 이런!
- You look terrible! 아주 안 좋아 보여요!
- I don't feel well. 기분이 안 좋아요. / 몸이 좋지 않아요.
- have a cold 감기에 걸리다
- have a headache 두통이 있다
- have a stomachache 배가 아프다
- feel better 몸이 나아지다
- sore 아픈, 쓰린
- symptom 증상
- have a runny nose 콧물이 흐르다
- have a sore throat 목이 아프다
- take medicine 약을 먹다
- What seems to be the problem? 어디가 아프십니까?
- take a look 보다
- aspirin 아스피린
- rest 휴식을 취하다

Get Ready

Look at the body parts. Write the names for as many body parts as you can.

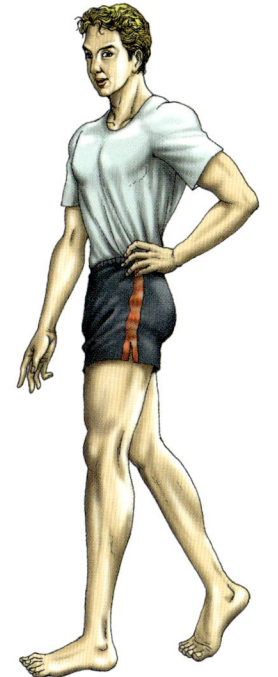
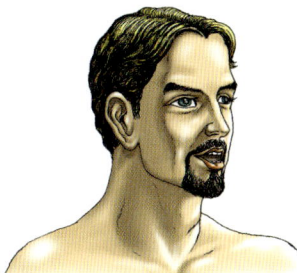

List of Body Parts

arm	ear	eye	nose	chest
head	mouth	neck	elbow	thumb
leg	toe	foot	ankle	knee
finger	hand	wrist	shoulder	chin
throat	stomach	back		

Conversation ❶   Being Sick

Track 52

Listen carefully. Then, practice the following conversation with your partner.

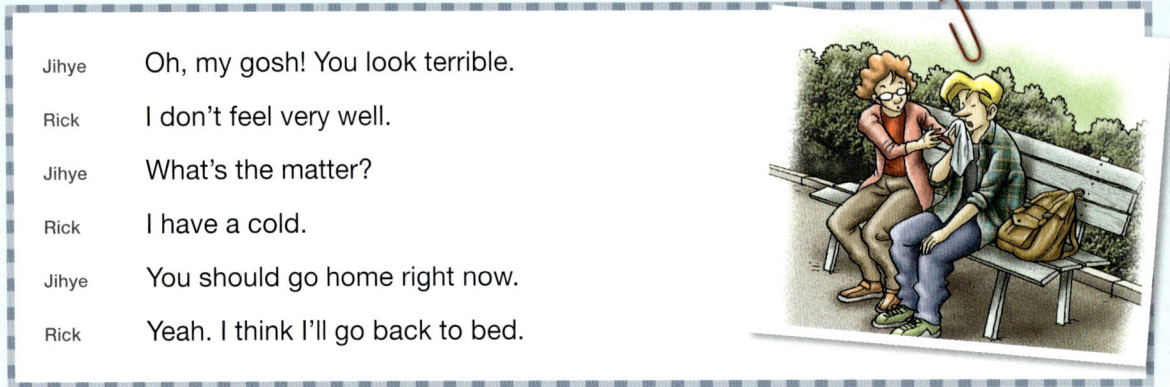

Jihye	Oh, my gosh! You look terrible.
Rick	I don't feel very well.
Jihye	What's the matter?
Rick	I have a cold.
Jihye	You should go home right now.
Rick	Yeah. I think I'll go back to bed.

Focus

A Look at the pictures and practice the expressions.

He has a cold.

He has a sore throat.

He has a fever.

He has insomnia.

He has a headache.

He has a stomachache.

He has a toothache.

He has a backache.

□ ache	□ sore	□ hurt
I have a/an _____.	I have a sore _____.	My _____ hurts.
headache	throat	eye
backache	arm	neck
stomachache	leg	leg
earache	knee	foot

140   English Communication 1

B *Match the explanations with the symptoms.*

1 John can't sleep at night. • • ⓐ He has insomnia.
2 Eunmi's head hurts a lot. • • ⓑ She is fatigued.
3 Kevin has a runny nose. • • ⓒ She has a fever.
4 Julie is tired all the time. • • ⓓ She has a stomachache.
5 Miss Lee's forehead is very hot. • • ⓔ He has an allergy problem.
6 Larry doesn't want to eat. • • ⓕ He has no appetite.
7 Chulsu's throat hurts. • • ⓖ She has a headache.
8 Angela is experiencing some stomach pain. • • ⓗ He has a sore throat.

C *Make sentences about each word. Use "ache," "sore," or "hurt."*

1 muscle   I have a muscle ache.
2 eye
3 toe
4 wrist
5 tooth
6 elbow
7 finger
8 heart
9 back
10 arm
11 ear
12 throat

Listen

Listen again. Then, complete the conversation.

Jihye: Oh, my gosh! You look _____.
Rick: I _____ very well.
Jihye: What's the _____?
Rick: I have a _____.
Jihye: You should go home right now.
Rick: Yeah. I think I'll go back to _____.

Conversation 2 Symptoms
Track 53

Listen carefully. Then, practice the following conversation with your partner.

Julie   Are you feeling better now?
Rick   Not really. I'm still sick.
Julie   What are your symptoms?
Rick   I have a runny nose and a sore throat.
Julie   Did you take any medicine?
Rick   Not yet. I'm going to the doctor soon.

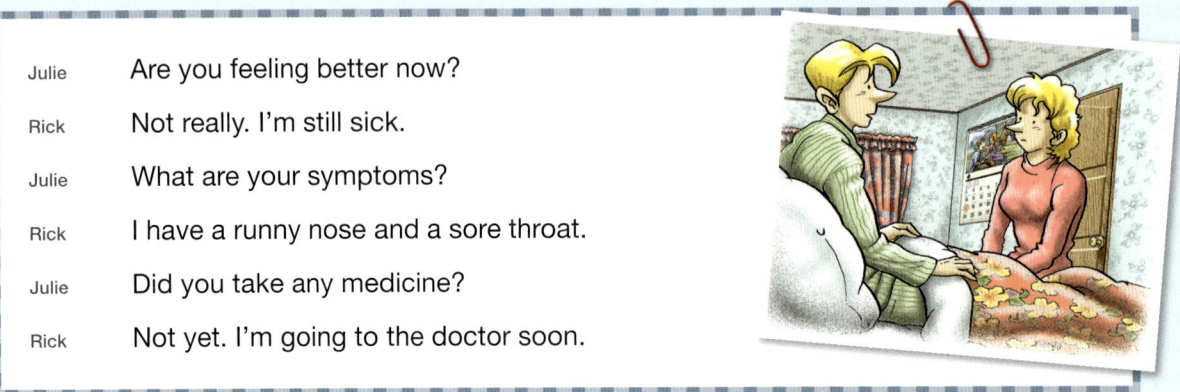

Focus

A Look at these common symptoms and practice the expressions.

I have _____.

- a runny nose
- a sore throat
- a fever
- a cough
- fatigue
- a stuffy nose
- the chills
- no appetite
- stomach pain
- a headache

B Look at the different health problems and diseases.
Which ones are health problems? Which ones are diseases? Make two lists.

- allergy
- blindness
- burn
- cut
- deafness
- dumb
- sprain
- pain
- stroke
- injury
- drug addiction
- swollen glands
- malaria
- AIDS
- the flu
- rash
- chicken pox
- food poisoning
- nausea
- cancer
- stiffness
- itch
- sore throat
- fever

Health Problems	Diseases

C Complete the sentences. Use the words in the box.

| food poisoning | cold | sprain | burn | ~~vomiting~~ | allergy |

1 John drank too much last night. He has a hangover, so he is __vomiting__ now.
2 Sumi hurt her wrist. She didn't break it, but she has a _____.
3 Mr. Park has a _____. His throat hurts, and he has a runny nose.
4 Lisa ate some bad food, so her stomach hurts. She has _____ now.
5 Minsu has a bad _____, so he can't stop sneezing.
6 Junga touched a very hot pot. She has a _____ on her hand.

Listen

Listen again. Then, complete the conversation.

Julie Are you _____ now?
Rick   Not really. I'm still _____.
Julie What are your _____?
Rick   I have a runny nose and a sore throat.
Julie Did you take any _____?
Rick   Not yet. I'm going to the _____ soon.

Your Turn to Speak

Talk to three other students. Ask them questions. Then, write the answers.

A What's wrong?
B I have a headache.

	Student ❶	Student ❷	Student ❸
a cold			
a stomachache			
a fatigue			

Conversation ③ Asking for and Giving Advice — Track 54

Listen carefully. Then, practice the following conversation with your partner.

Doctor	What seems to be the problem?
Rick	I think I have a cold.
Doctor	Hmm. Let me take a look.
Rick	What should I do?
Doctor	You should take some aspirin. And you should go to bed and rest.
Rick	Thanks, Doc.

Focus

A Look at this common advice and practice the expressions.

- see a doctor 의사에게 진찰을 받다
- take some aspirin 아스피린을 복용하다
- take some vitamin C 비타민 C를 복용하다
- avoid spicy foods 자극적인 음식을 피하다
- use a heating pad 찜질 패드를 사용하다
- see a dentist 치과에서 진찰을 받다
- take some cough drops 기침약을 복용하다
- drink lots of liquids 음료수를 많이 마시다
- go to bed and rest 잠자리에서 편히 쉬다

B Give advice for these problems.

1. I have a sore throat. → You should _drink warm water._
2. I have a headache. → You should _____.
3. Minhee has a cold. → She should _____.
4. James has a burn. → He should _____.
5. I have a toothache. → You need to _____.
6. Sumi is fatigued. → She needs to _____.
7. I have a fever. → You ought to _____.
8. Mr. Jones has insomnia. → He ought to _____.
9. I have a cough. → You ought to _____.
10. Minho has a bloody nose. → He ought to _____.

C Complete the expressions. Use the words in the box.

| visit | ~~see~~ | listen | take |
| not go | not drink | not worry | not eat |

1 __see__ a dentist
2 _____ too much
3 _____ some aspirin
4 _____ to work/school
5 _____ to classical music
6 _____ a doctor
7 _____ beer
8 _____ any junk food

D Read the article. Then, talk about the questions with your partner.

How Healthy Are You?

You can't buy good health at the drugstore. And visiting the doctor doesn't always help either. You need to take care of your body so that you don't have any major problems. If you have bad habits and don't visit the doctor, you will have many problems in the future.

You need to understand your own body. Everyone gets in accidents. No one can avoid certain diseases. But a poor diet, stress, and a bad working environment plus not exercising enough can ruin your health. If you change your habits and your environment, you can lower the risk of getting sick and reduce the damage from disease.

1 How often do you exercise every week?
2 What kinds of exercises do you regularly do?
3 Do you try to be healthy?
4 How do you stay healthy?
5 How physically fit are you?

Listen

Listen again. Then, complete the conversation.

Doctor   What seems to be _____?

Rick   I think I have a _____.

Doctor   Hmm. Let me _____ a _____.

Rick   What should I do?

Doctor   You should _____ some aspirin. And you should go to bed and _____.

Rick   Thanks, Doc.

Your Turn to Speak

Talk to three other students. Tell them about your problems. Then, ask them for advice. Write the answers.

A: I have the flu. What should I do?
B: You should take some medicine.

	Student ❶	Student ❷	Student ❸
the flu			
a cough			
insomnia			
a backache			

 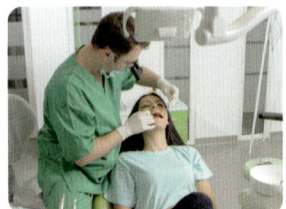  

Let's Practice Pronunciation

Track 55

Pronunciation

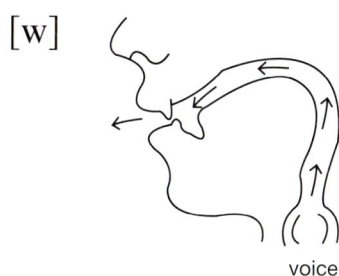

[w]

voice

Word Comparison

Try pronouncing the words below.

[w]	went	wine	wimp	wash	wet	wise	west	wiper	wall
	always	allow	away	stow	row	grow	distinguish	language	once

Sentences

Read the following sentences. Try to pronounce [w] correctly.

1 **Who** got the vet **wet**?
2 **We swam** in the **waves** on the **west** coast on **Wednesday**.
3 **Wendy washed** the **window** while **Wayne** slept.
4 The **wise** queen **was aware** of the **woman's wish**.
5 **I wonder why Webster** moved **away** from the **White** River.

Sentence Patterns

1 You look _____.

   terrible | gorgeous | great

   너 _____ 해 보인다.

   안 좋은 | 굉장히 멋진 | 아주 좋은

2 I have _____.

   a runny nose | a sore throat | insomnia

   나는 _____ 한 증세가 있어.

   콧물 | 목 아픔 | 불면증

3 You should _____.

   get some rest
   take some aspirin
   see a doctor

   _____ 하는 게 좋습니다.

   휴식을 취하다
   아스피린을 복용하다
   의사에게 진찰을 받다

Let's Read

Going to the Doctor

Hospital vs. Doctor

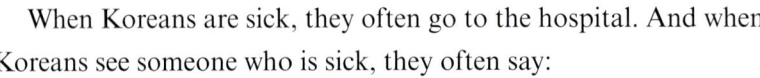

When Koreans are sick, they often go to the hospital. And when Koreans see someone who is sick, they often say:

> You should go to the hospital.
> You need to go to the hospital.
> You ought to go to the hospital.

However, when you say this to an American, he might be surprised. The reason is that most Americans only go to the hospital for an emergency. When Americans are sick, they often go to a doctor's clinic or someplace small, not a hospital.

So, if you say, "You should go to the hospital," don't be surprised if the person answers, "That's okay. I'm not that sick," or, "I don't need a hospital." To make sure the foreigner understands what you mean, you should say:

> You should see a doctor.
> You should visit the doctor.
> You should go to a clinic.

If you use these expressions, the person should completely understand you.

Let's Talk More

1. Where do you go when you are sick?
2. What happened the last time you went to the doctor? Talk about it.
3. Do you have a funny story about visiting the doctor? Can you tell it?

UNIT 15 I will take a trip this summer.

Vocabulary

- **I will ~** 나는 ~할 거야
- **take a trip** 여행을 가다
- **equipment** 장비, 도구
- **baggage** 짐, 수하물
- **travel document** 여행 서류
- **Of course.** 물론이지.
- **What will you do?** 무엇을 할 거예요?
- **go shopping** 쇼핑하러 가다
- **What are your plans?** 계획이 뭐예요?
- **I am going to ~** 나는 ~할 거야
- **Tell me about it.** 그러게 말이야.
- **What are you going to do?** 무엇을 할 거예요?
- **clearly** 명확하게
- **vacation** 방학

Get Ready

Read the words in the box. Underline the words you don't know.
Then, ask your teacher about these words.

- passport
- cash
- backpack
- sleeping bag
- bathing suit
- travel insurance
- traveler's checks
- visa
- airplane ticket
- suitcase
- credit card
- first-aid kit
- fanny pack
- shorts
- underwear
- smartphone
- international driver's license
- briefcase
- digital camera
- video camera

Conversation 1 The Future with "Will" ⊙ Track 56

Listen carefully. Then, practice the following conversation with your partner.

Sungmin Why do you look so happy today?
Julie Summer vacation is coming.
Sungmin Right. What will you do this summer?
Julie I will take a trip this summer.
Sungmin That's great. Where are you going?
Julie I'm going to Australia next week.

Focus

A You will take a trip. What do you need? Write each word from "Get Ready" in the correct category. Then, add two more words to each category.

Money	Equipment	Baggage	Clothing	Travel Documents
cash				

B Find a partner. Choose the five most important items you need to travel to another country. Explain why you need to take them on your trip.

_____

_____

_____

_____

_____

C *Form a group. Tell the group about your important items. Do you agree or disagree?*

_____
_____
_____
_____
_____

D *Complete the sentences by using "will."*

The future with "will": will + verb

do → will do	go → will go	eat → will eat
have → will have	hire → will hire	learn → will learn
make → will make	stay → will stay	study → will study
take → will take	talk → will talk	write → will write

1 (see) After class, I *will see a movie.*
2 (do) This evening, I _____.
3 (study) Tomorrow, we _____.
4 (write) Tomorrow morning, I _____.
5 (meet) This Friday, I _____.
6 (talk) This weekend, my friend and I _____.
7 (learn) Next week, I _____.

Listen

Listen again. Then, complete the conversation.

Sungmin Why do you _____ so happy today?

Julie Summer vacation is _____.

Sungmin Right. What _____ this summer?

Julie I _____ this summer.

Sungmin That's great. Where are you going?

Julie I'm going to Australia next week.

Conversation 2 — Future Actions

Track 57

Listen carefully. Then, practice the following conversation with your partner.

Sumi	What are you doing this evening?
Jihye	I will go shopping with my boyfriend.
Sumi	Your boyfriend likes shopping?
Jihye	No, he hates it. But he will go with me.
Sumi	Wow. He must really love you.
Jihye	I think so.

Focus

A Look at the forms of the future tense.

will

- Use **will** + **verb** when you suddenly decide to do something.
    The telephone is ringing. → Okay. I **will answer** it.
    John can't find his jacket. → We **will help** him.

- Use **will** when you talk about the future.
    It's six o'clock. I **will go** home at eight.

- Contraction
    I will = I'll   you will = you'll   he will = he'll   she will = she'll
    it will = it'll   we will = we'll   they will = they'll   will not = won't

Future Time Expressions

- tonight
- tomorrow
- tomorrow morning / tomorrow evening
- this Monday / this week
- next Tuesday / next week
- soon
- later

- in a while
- in two days (= two days from now)
- in three weeks (= three weeks from now)
- in a few minutes
- in the future
- around midnight
- at nine o'clock

B *Match the sentences with the answers.*

1 Someone is knocking at the door. •   • ⓐ I'll take it to the vet.
2 I'm thirsty.   •   • ⓑ Don't worry. I'll help you.
3 I can't do this math problem.   •   • ⓒ I'll fix it for you.
4 The dog hurt its leg.   •   • ⓓ I'll get you a drink.
5 I broke my bike.   •   • ⓔ I'll find out who it is.

C *Complete the sentences. Use "will" or "won't" plus the verbs in the box.*

have	take	phone	finish	be	do	make

1 A Are you going to the movies on Sunday?
   B I'm not sure. I ___will phone___ you on Sunday.
2 A Don't change your clothes now. We _____ late.
   B No, we won't. We _____ a taxi.
3 A Bob _____ a party this week.
   B Why?
   A It's his birthday.
4 A She _____ well on her test tomorrow.
   B Why not?
   A She _____ some mistakes. She always makes mistakes.
5 A _____ Kevin _____ the work tonight?
   B No, he won't.

D *Ask your partner questions. Then, write the answers.*

A	What will you do tomorrow at 7:00 A.M.?
B	I will go for a walk.

What will you do tomorrow at _____?

▫ 7:00 A.M.   ▫ 10:00 A.M.
▫ 12:00 P.M.   ▫ 2:00 P.M.
▫ 5:00 P.M.   ▫ 6:00 P.M.
▫ 9:00 P.M.   ▫ 11:00 P.M.

E *Write the answers about yourself.*

1. What will you do tomorrow at 8:00 A.M.?
   _____

2. What will you do tomorrow at 12:00 P.M.?
   _____

3. What will you do tomorrow at 5:00 P.M.?
   _____

4. What will you do this weekend?
   _____

5. What will you do this summer vacation?
   _____

6. What will you eat tonight?
   _____

7. Who will you meet tomorrow?
   _____

8. Where will you go this weekend?
   _____

9. When will you take a break?
   _____

10. When will you go online?
    _____

Listen

Listen again. Then, complete the conversation.

Sumi	What are you _____ this evening?
Jihye	I _____ shopping with my boyfriend.
Sumi	Your boyfriend _____?
Jihye	No, he _____ it. But he will go with me.
Sumi	Wow. He must really love you.
Jihye	I think so.

Conversation 3 — The Future with "Be Going To"

 Track 58

Listen carefully. Then, practice the following conversation with your partner.

Rick	What are your plans for today?
Julie	I'm going to go to the library.
Rick	Why? Are you going to study?
Julie	Of course. And then I'm going to have dinner with Sungmin.
Rick	You're going to be very busy today.
Julie	Tell me about it.

Focus

A Look at the forms below and practice them.

> **be going to**
>
> Use **be going to** + **verb** when you talk about the future or something you will definitely do.
> **I am going to study** hard tonight.
> They **are going to eat** dinner soon.
>
> [Positive]   [Negative]
> I **am going to** leave.   I **am not going to** leave.
> He **is going to** leave.   He **is not going to** leave.
> We **are going to** leave.   We **are not going to** leave.

B Complete the sentences by using "be going to." Use the verbs in parentheses.

1. I ___am going to study___ hard this semester. (study)
2. He _____ all over the world. (travel)
3. She _____ in an office. (not work)
4. They _____ next year. (graduate)
5. We _____ a great time. (have)
6. She _____ to her friends. (not talk)
7. I _____ Tina at the shopping mall. (meet)
8. We _____ seafood tonight. (not eat)

C *Answer the questions.*

1 What are your plans for today? _____
2 What are you going to do this weekend? _____
3 What are you going to do next week? _____
4 Where are you going to go tomorrow? _____
5 What movie are you going to see soon? _____

Listen

Listen again. Then, complete the conversation.

Rick   What are your plans for today?
Julie   _____ go to the library.
Rick   Why? _____ study?
Julie   Of course. And then _____ dinner with Sungmin.
Rick   _____ very busy today.
Julie: Tell me about it.

Your Turn to Speak

Talk to three other students. Ask them questions. Then, write the answers.

A What are you going to eat tonight?
B I'm going to eat spaghetti.

	Student ❶	Student ❷	Student ❸
eat tonight			
watch on TV later			
buy on the weekend			
talk about later			

Let's Practice Pronunciation

Track 59

Pronunciation

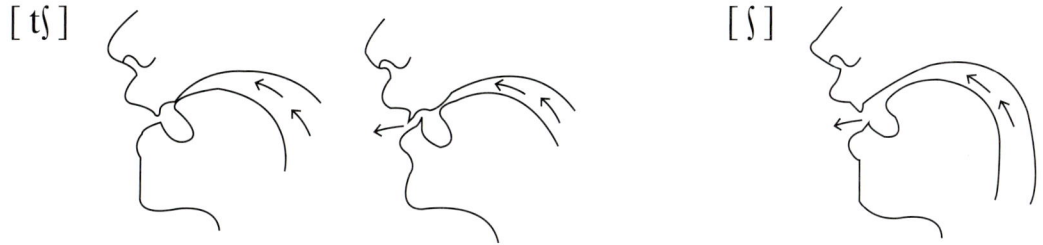

Word Comparison

[tʃ] and [ʃ] have different sounds. Try pronouncing the words below.

[tʃ]	chock	chip	chin	chew	witch	ditch	chatter	choose	watch	match
[ʃ]	shock	ship	shin	shoe	wish	dish	shatter	shoes	wash	mash

Sentences

Read the following sentences. Try to pronounce [tʃ] and [ʃ] correctly.

1. There's a **cherry** in my **sherry**!
2. This **shirt** and **sheet** will **shrink** in the **washer**.
3. I **chipped** my **shin** and **shattered** the bone.
4. He **crushes** his **crutches**.
5. The dog likes to **chew shoes**.

Sentence Patterns

1. Why do you look so _____ today?
   happy | angry | excited

   오늘 왜 그렇게 _____ 해 보이니?
   행복한 | 화난 | 신난

2. I will _____ with my boyfriend.
   go shopping | go on a trip | go for a walk

   나는 남자친구와 _____ 할 거야.
   쇼핑하러 가다 | 여행가다 | 산책하러 가다

3. I'm going to go _____.
   to the library | to school | home

   나는 _____ 갈 예정이야.
   도서관에 | 학교에 | 집에

Let's Read

Time Expressions

Speak Clearly with Time Words

When you talk about the future, you always need to use time expressions. If you don't use a time expression, the person won't know when exactly you are talking about. For example, you might say, "I will meet my friend." That is perfect English, but you need to use a time expression; otherwise, you might confuse the person you are speaking with.

Don't just say, "I will meet my friend." Instead, say:

> I will meet my friend soon.
> I will meet my friend tonight.
> I will meet my friend this weekend.

There are many different time expressions to use. So it's very important that you identify the time.

In addition, in many cases, the position of the time expression in the sentence is NOT that important. In the above sentences, the time expression is last. However, you can often put the time expression at the beginning of the sentence. You can say:

> Soon, I will meet my friend.
> Tonight, I will meet my friend.
> This weekend, I will meet my friend.

Put them at the end or the beginning. But just be sure that you use time expressions.

Let's Talk More

1. What are some future time expressions?
2. Do you always use future time expressions when you speak?
3. What are some present and past time expressions?

UNIT 16 I want to be a businesswoman.

Vocabulary

- think about ~에 대해서 생각하다
- What do you want to be? 무엇이 되고 싶어요?
- in the future 미래에
- I'm not sure. 잘 모르겠어. / 확실치 않아.
- businesswoman 여성 사업가
- successful 성공한
- the last year of school 마지막 학년
- be worried about ~에 대해서 걱정하다
- graduate 졸업하다
- get a job 취직하다
- office 사무실
- sales 판매
- responsibility 책임
- sell 팔다
- product 상품
- retire 은퇴하다, 퇴직하다

Get Ready

Look at the list. Then, talk to your classmates. What are they doing next week?

Find Someone Who Is ~	Name	Follow-up Questions	Answers
playing sports		What are you playing?	
doing an outdoor activity		What are you doing?	
going shopping		Where are you going?	
going somewhere interesting		Where are you going?	
hanging out with friends		Who are you hanging out with?	
eating tasty food		Where are you going?	

Conversation ❶ Future Plans — ◉ Track 60

Listen carefully. Then, practice the following conversation with your partner.

Minhee: What are you thinking about?
Sungmin: I'm thinking about my future.
Minhee: Really? What do you want to be in the future?
Sungmin: I'm not sure now.
Minhee: I want to be a businesswoman.
Sungmin: I'm sure that you'll be successful.

Focus

A Ask your partner questions. Then, write the answers.

In the future, what do you want to _____?
▫ be   ▫ do

In the future, where do you want to _____?
▫ live
▫ work
▫ go on your honeymoon
▫ live when you retire

B Answer the questions about yourself.

1. In the future, what do you want to be? _In the future, I want to be a teacher._
2. In the future, what do you want to do? _____
3. In the future, where do you want to live? _____
4. In the future, where do you want to work? _____
5. In the future, when do you want to get married? _____
6. In the future, when do you want to have children? _____
7. In ten years, what do you want to do? _____
8. In twenty years, what do you want to do? _____

C Think about your life in twenty years. What do you want your life to be like? Make sentences about the different topics.

1 job   In twenty years, I want to be a businesswoman.
2 husband / wife _____
3 children   _____
4 money   _____
5 hobby   _____
6 free-time activity _____

Listen

Listen again. Then, complete the conversation.

Minhee   What are you thinking about?
Sungmin I'm thinking about my _____.
Minhee   Really? What do you _____ in the _____?
Sungmin I'm not sure now.
Minhee   I want to be a businesswoman.
Sungmin I'm sure that you'll be _____.

Your Turn to Speak

Talk to three other students. Ask them questions. Then, write the answers.

A In the future, ~?

- What do you want to be?
- What kind of person do you want to marry?
- What hobby do you want to have?
- Where do you want to go on vacation?

	Student ❶	Student ❷	Student ❸
job			
marriage			
hobby			
vacation			

Conversation 2 — Using "After"

Track 61

Listen carefully. Then, practice the following conversation with your partner.

Rick	It's my last year of school. I'm worried about my future.
Sumi	After you graduate, what are you going to do?
Rick:	Hmm... After graduating, I'm going to get a job.
Sumi	Where do you want to work?
Rick	I'm not sure yet. I have to think about it.
Sumi	I'm positive that you'll find a good job soon.

Focus

A Ask your partner questions. Then, write the answers.

After _____, what are you going to do?

- you finish class
- the workweek finishes
- graduating
- meeting your friends this weekend
- you go home
- the semester ends
- waking up tomorrow
- getting married

B Combine the two actions into one sentence by using "before" or "after."

I put on my jacket. I went outside.
(before) Before I went outside, I put on my jacket.
(after)   After I put on my jacket, I went outside.

1 We bought tickets. We entered the movie theater.
   (before) _____
   (after) _____

2 She ate breakfast. She went to school.
   (before) _____
   (after) _____

3 I finished dinner. I watched TV.

   (before) _____

   (after) _____

4 He did his homework. He went out with his girlfriend.

   (before) _____

   (after) _____

5 They studied at the library. They took a test.

   (before) _____

   (after) _____

C *Circle the mistakes. Then, write the correct sentences.*

1 After I (graduating), I will find a job.
   → After I graduate, I will find a job.

2 Mary meets her friends tonight after she finishes class.
   → _____

3 Sumi and Jihye are going to watch a movie after her workday is over.
   → _____

4 After take this test, we are going to have dinner.
   → _____

5 After I get paid, I'm going buy my girlfriend a nice present.
   → _____

Listen

Listen again. Then, complete the conversation.

Rick   It's my last year of school. I'm _____ about my future.

Sumi   After you _____, what are you going to do?

Rick   Hmm... _____ graduating, I'm going to get a job.

Sumi   Where do you want to work?

Rick   I'm not sure yet. I have to think about it.

Sumi   I'm positive that you'll _____ a good job soon.

Conversation 3 — Job Descriptions

Track 62

Listen carefully. Then, practice the following conversation with your partner.

Jihye	Why are you smiling so much? Do you have good news?
Julie	No, I have great news. I just got a job!
Jihye	That's wonderful. Where are you working now?
Julie	I'm working in an office. I'm in sales.
Jihye	Sales? What are your job responsibilities?
Julie	I have to sell my company's products. And I do other things, too.

Focus

A Look at the different jobs.

- salesman
- businessman
- secretary
- receptionist
- manager
- architect
- doctor
- nurse
- taxi driver
- engineer
- manager
- director
- editor
- writer
- reporter
- tour guide
- translator
- designer
- programmer
- police officer
- soldier
- mechanic
- accountant
- public relations officer

B Look at the different job responsibilities.

- sell products
- file papers
- answer the telephone
- take messages
- meet clients
- design buildings
- write computer programs
- drive passengers
- go on business trips
- take care of patients
- conduct research
- cook meals
- write reports
- manage employees
- enforce the law
- edit papers

C *Match each department with the correct job responsibility.*

1. Sales — ⓒ sell a company's products
2. Marketing — ⓕ help promote a company's products
3. Accounting — ⓐ control a company's money
4. Human Resources — ⓑ find and hire new employees
5. Research — ⓓ try to create new products
6. Customer Relations — ⓔ be responsible for public relations

D *Complete the sentences. Use the words and expressions in the boxes above.*

1. Sumi is a _____nurse_____. She takes care of patients.
2. Mark is a _____. He drives passengers around the city.
3. Sungmin is a _____. He fixes cars and trucks.
4. Eungyoung is an _____. She edits books and papers.
5. Minho is a police officer. He _____.
6. Mr. Smith is an architect. He _____.
7. Julie is a businesswoman. She _____.
8. Sangmi is a programmer. She _____.

E *Write "true" or "false."*

1. A secretary takes care of patients.   _____
2. An architect designs buildings.   _____
3. A receptionist answers the telephone.   _____
4. A translator writes computer programs.   _____
5. A soldier sells products.   _____
6. A director manages employees.   _____

F *Fill in the blanks. Use the words in the box.*

chef	programmer	translator	doctor

Rick is graduating soon. After he graduates, he wants to find a job. But he doesn't know what he should do. He likes computers, so maybe he will become a (1) _____. But he also wants to help people, so he could become a (2) _____. He hates cooking, so he won't become a (3) _____. And he doesn't speak any foreign languages, so he can't become a (4) _____. Before he graduates, he needs to choose a job.

Listen

Listen again. Then, complete the conversation.

Jihye   Why are you smiling so much? Do you have good news?
Julie   No, I have great news. I just got a _____!
Jihye   That's wonderful. Where are you working now?
Julie   I'm working in an _____. I'm in _____.
Jihye   Sales? What are your job responsibilities?
Julie   I have to _____ my company's products. And I do other things, too.

Your Turn to Speak

Talk to three other students. Ask them questions. Then, write the answers.

A What is your job?
B I am an office worker.
A What is one of your job responsibilities?
B I answer the telephone.

	Student ❶	Student ❷	Student ❸
Job			
Responsibility 1			
Responsibility 2			
Responsibility 3			

Let's Practice Pronunciation

Track 63

Pronunciation

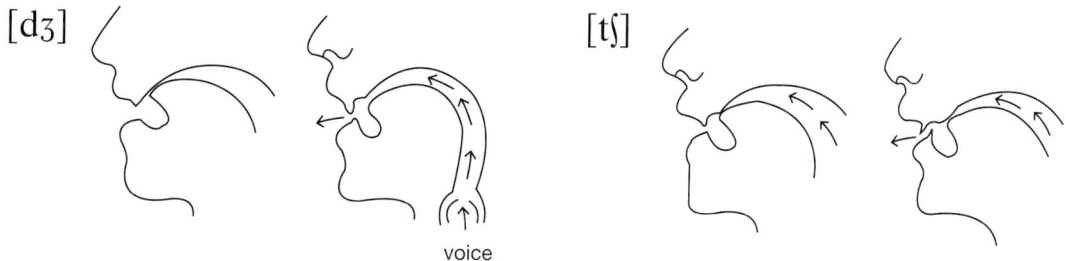

Word Comparison

[dʒ] and [tʃ] have different sounds. Try pronouncing the words below.

[dʒ]	jug	juice	Jew	junk	jest	joke	bridges	large	edge	ridge
[tʃ]	chug	choose	chew	chunk	chest	choke	britches	latch	etch	rich

Sentences

Read the following sentences. Try to pronounce [dʒ] and [tʃ] correctly.

1 **Each child chose** his own **jelly**.
2 They found many **riches** in those **ridges**.
3 **Jack injured** his **chin**, **jaw**, and **chest**.
4 He **searched** for his blue **jacket**.
5 **Jenny** likes **kimchi**, **cheese**, and **peaches**.

Sentence Patterns

1 What are you _____ about?
   thinking | talking | arguing

   무엇에 대해 ____ 하고 있니?
   생각하고 | 얘기하고 | 논의하고

2 After graduating, I'm going to _____.
   get a job | go abroad to study | get married

   졸업한 후에 나는 ____ 할 거야.
   취업하다 | 유학가다 | 결혼하다

3 I'm working in _____.
   an office | a hospital | a software company

   나는 ____ 에서 일하고 있어요.
   사무실 | 병원 | 소프트웨어 회사

Unit 16 I want to be a businesswoman.

Let's Read

Saying Goodbye
Different Ways to Say Goodbye

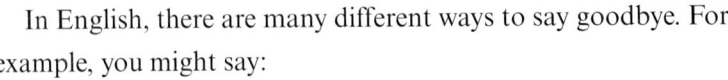

In English, there are many different ways to say goodbye. For example, you might say:

Goodbye.
See you later.
Take it easy.

There are so many expressions. However, we use these expressions in many different ways. For example, "Goodbye" is probably the most formal expression to say to someone when you are leaving. You should use this in formal situations (like at work), but you probably don't use this with your friends. (However, this is the best expression to use when you end a phone call.) Also, you might say "Goodbye" to a person when you think that you won't see him or her for a long time.

When you are saying farewell to your friends, there are many different expressions you can use. Of course, you are probably going to be more informal. Some more informal goodbyes are:

Bye bye.
See you. (See ya.)
Later.

You can use all of these in more casual situations. And some of the most common goodbyes are "See you later," "See you tomorrow," "See you at 6," and "See you next week."

And now that our book is ending, it's time for us to say goodbye. See you next semester!

Let's Talk More

1. What are some different ways to say goodbye?
2. Do you enjoy saying goodbye? Why or why not?

Appendix

→ **Answer Key**

→ **Listen**

→ **How to Pronounce Each Sound**

Answer Key

Unit 01 | It's nice to meet you.

Conversation 1

C 1 ⓕ   2 ⓖ   3 ⓐ   4 ⓑ
   5 ⓔ   6 ⓓ   7 ⓒ

Conversation 3

C (1) favorite   (2) enjoy
   (3) How   (4) best
   (5) love

Unit 02 | What are you doing now?

Get Ready

2 is talking   3 are doing
4 is meeting   5 are having
6 are taking

Conversation 1

A 2 watching a movie   3 swimming
   4 studying   5 playing basketball
   6 cooking   7 playing the flute
   8 riding a bicycle   9 jogging

B 2 We are exercising at the gym.
   3 My sister is studying for her English test.
   4 They are playing computer games now.
   5 He is talking to his girlfriend now.
   6 Mr. Park and Mr. Lee are having a meeting
   7 John is meeting a client now.
   8 What are they eating right now?

D 2 It's two o'clock. / It's 2 P.M. (A.M.)
   3 It's seven fifteen. / It's fifteen past seven.
   4 It's noon. / It's midnight.
   5 It's nine fifty-five. / It's five to ten.
   6 It's eight ten. / It's ten past eight.

Conversation 3

B 2 am playing computer games
   3 am going to my office
   4 is meeting me
   5 is calling me

Unit 03 | Where is it?

Conversation 1

A 1 on   2 behind
   3 in front of   4 far from
   5 next to   6 near
   7 across from   8 on the corner of

B 1 The hospital is on Western Avenue.
   2 The supermarket is across from the school.
   3 The library is near the rental car agency.
   4 The bookstore is next to the park.
   5 The shopping center is on the corner of Douglas Drive and Eastern Avenue.
   6 The hotel is across from the hospital.
   7 The bar is near the office building.
   8 The restaurant is next to the electronics store.

Conversation 2

B 1 false   2 true
   3 false   4 false
   5 true   6 false
   7 true

Conversation 3

A 1 7   2 7
   3 4   4 Gangnam
   5 Jamsil   6 Sindorim

B 1 ⓒ   2 ⓐ   3 ⓔ   4 ⓓ
   5 ⓑ

Unit 04 | What do you usually do after school?

Get Ready

1 in   2 on   3 at   4 in
5 on   6 at   7 on   8 at
9 in   10 on   11 in   12 in

Conversation 2

A 2 ⓐ   3 ⓒ   4 ⓑ   5 ⓔ
   6 ⓖ   7 ⓕ

170 English Communication 1

C 2 I often have coffee, scrambled eggs, and pancakes.
3 Do you usually eat breakfast at work?
4 I sometimes have breakfast at my desk.
5 Do you usually eat a bowl of rice for breakfast?
6 No, I hardly ever have rice.

D 2 What do you usually do after school?
3 I often brush my teeth.
4 Lisa never studies hard.
5 Do you always watch action movies?
6 What do they usually study?
7 He always/sometimes surfs the Internet.

Conversation 3

D 2 Sumi sometimes takes a trip.
3 My brother usually plays soccer.
4 Mr. Park seldom washes his car.
5 Scott always calls his girlfriend.
6 Ms. Han sometimes cooks.

Unit 05 | Can you tell me about your family?

Conversation 1

B 1 mother (parent)   2 son
3 father   4 parents
5 uncles   6 aunt
7 grandchild (granddaughter)
8 nephew   9 cousin
10 nieces

Conversation 2

A 1 ⓓ   2 ⓖ   3 ⓗ   4 ⓕ
5 ⓔ   6 ⓑ   7 ⓐ   8 ⓒ

B 2 A nurse takes care of sick people.
3 A professor teaches at a university or college.
4 A firefighter puts out fires.
5 An artist makes art.
6 A businessperson works for a company.

C 1 secretary   2 plumber
3 taxi driver   4 lawyer
5 maid   6 congressman

D 1 goes   2 works
3 is   4 has
5 helps   6 rides
7 sells   8 cooks

E 1 work, walk, doesn't, rides
2 live, takes, doesn't, uses, doesn't

Conversation 3

A 1 in her teens   2 in her twenties
3 is his early thirties 4 in her mid-forties
5 in his late fifties   6 in her seventies

B 1 false   2 true
3 true   4 true
5 false

Unit 06 | What do you like?

Conversation 2

B 3 David loves to drive his car.
4 The students are crazy about English.
5 Miss Kim loves going on trips.
6 Larry is crazy about playing sports.
7 The childen are crazy.
8 I love shopping online.

C (1) having   (2) sitting
(3) making   (4) playing
(5) lying   (6) reading
(7) listening   (8) watching
(9) visiting   (10) being

D 2 Mr. and Mrs. Taylor like driving their car.
3 I like watching (to watch) sports on television.
4 The students like doing homework very much.
5 He is crazy about his girlfriend.
6 Chris likes going out with his friends.
7 Mr. Park loves his wife very much.
8 I like my job very much.
9 Wendy is crazy about her new puppy.
10 Do you like buying new clothes?

Conversation 3

C 1 Does Sally like driving her car? / No, she hates driving her car.
2 Do Bob and Steve like eating fried chicken? / Yes, they like eating fried chicken.
3 Does Mr. Lee like cleaning the house? / No, he does not like cleaning the house.
4 Does the baby like taking medicine? / No, it hates taking medicine.
5 Do the children like watching TV? / Yes, they like watching TV.

6 Does Kate like doing her homework? /
Do, she dislikes doing her homework.
7 Does Sam like getting up early? /
No, he hates getting up early.

Unit 07 | What's he like?

Conversation ①

A 1 ⓔ   2 ⓐ   3 ⓖ   4 ⓑ
   5 ⓓ   6 ⓗ   7 ⓒ   8 ⓕ

Conversation ②

A 2 ⓘ   3 ⓗ   4 ⓑ   5 ⓕ
   6 ⓓ   7 ⓒ   8 ⓚ   9 ⓔ
   10 ⓛ   11 ⓐ   12 ⓙ

B 1 at/with   2 of
   3 of   4 about
   5 with/about   6 in/by/with
   7 about   8 about

Conversation ③

A 2 bad   3 bad
   4 good   5 bad
   6 bad   7 bad
   8 good

B 1 jealous   2 depressed
   3 lonely   4 exhausted
   5 shocked   6 disgusted
   7 anxious   8 embarrassed

D 2 stop drinking beer every night
   3 lose weight
   4 go to bed early
   5 should smile
   6 should not talk too much
   7 needs to be polite
   8 should not get angry

Unit 08 | What does she look like?

Conversation ②

B 1 ⓑ   2 ⓔ   3 ⓒ   4 ⓐ
   5 ⓓ   6 ⓗ   7 ⓕ   8 ⓖ

Conversation ③

B 1 ⓑ   2 ⓔ   3 ⓒ   4 ⓐ
   5 ⓓ

C 2 casual   3 formal
   4 casual   6 formal
   7 casual   8 formal

Unit 09 | I can do it.

Conversation ②

A 1 ⓑ   2 ⓕ   3 ⓓ   4 ⓗ
   5 ⓔ   6 ⓖ   7 ⓒ   8 ⓐ

C 2 cannot fly   3 cannot climb a tree
   4 can float on water 5 cannot run fast
   6 can read a book

Conversation ③

D 2 I can play baseball very well.
   3 Miss Smith is able to travel to many different places.
   4 William cannot drive a bus.
   5 The teacher ought to come to school early.
   6 She must call me very soon.

E 1 have to   2 ought to
   3 ought to   4 must
   5 has to   6 must
   7 should   8 have to

Unit 10 | What did you do yesterday?

Conversation ①

B 1 cleaned   2 watched
   3 climbed   4 played
   5 arrived   6 returned
   7 lied   8 studied
   9 stopped   10 started
   11 married   12 loved

C 2 When did you go?
   3 Where did you stay?
   4 Who did you go with?
   5 How long did you stay?
   6 What did you do?

7 Whom did you meet?
8 What did you buy?

Conversation 2

B 2 saw   3 put
   4 came   5 ate
   6 sat   7 wrote

Conversation 3

C 2 last   3 yesterday
   4 ago   5 yesterday
   6 last   7 ago
   8 yesterday/last

D 1 ⓑ   2 ⓔ   3 ⓓ   4 ⓖ
   5 ⓕ   6 ⓒ   7 ⓐ

E (1) waited   (2) didn't call
   (3) stayed   (4) watched
   (5) visited   (6) talked
   (7) listened   (8) invited
   (9) cooked   (10) didn't work
   (11) didn't study

F 1 Who did you meet two days ago?
   2 They played a game this morning.
   3 They moved to a new home last year.
   4 I slept for eight hours last night.
   5 What did you do last weekend?
   6 Mr. Smith called me five minutes ago.
   7 I ate breakfast at 7:00 this morning.
   8 We brought our lunches to school yesterday.

Unit 11 | I had long hair when I was young.

Conversation 1

A 1 ⓒ   2 ⓓ   3 ⓔ   4 ⓑ
   5 ⓕ   6 ⓐ   7 ⓗ   8 ⓖ

D 1 What did you study after lunch?
   2 Why didn't you go to class?
   3 When did the baseball game begin?
   4 Where did your wife go?
   5 When did you meet him?

Conversation 3

D 2 ⓓ   3 ⓗ   4 ⓐ   5 ⓑ
   6 ⓔ   7 ⓕ   8 ⓒ

E 1 Where did Jason use to live?
   2 Kyoungmi used to work in a hospital.
   3 Trevor used to read books every day.
   4 What did you use to play as a child?
   5 He used to be bad, but now he is nice.
   6 Did you use to play the piano?

F (1) be   (2) study
   (3) ride   (4) play
   (5) cook   (6) like

Unit 12 | How about going out tonight?

Conversation 1

A 2 study   3 take
   4 go   5 do
   6 clean   7 buy

B 1 Let's go to a concert.
   2 Let's eat.
   3 Let's leave at eight thirty.
   4 Let's go to Hawaii.

Conversation 2

C 2 How about watching a movie with me?
   3 What should we do tonight?
   4 Let's have dinner together.
   5 I'd love to go to the park with you.
   6 Would you like to meet me later tonight?

Conversation 3

B 1 ⓑ   2 ⓓ   3 ⓔ   4 ⓒ
   5 ⓐ

C 1 Hi. Is Sangmi there? / No, she's not here.
   2 Hi. Is Mr. Lee around? / Yes, hold on, please.
   3 Hello. May I speak to Lisa, please? /
     Sorry. She's busy now.
   4 Hi. Is Amy there? / Yes, just a minute, please.

D (1) May   (2) Sorry
   (3) message   (4) Sure
   (5) ask   (6) give
   (7) Bye

Unit 13 | I want to see a movie.

Conversation 1

C 1 visit - ⓒ   2 attend - ⓑ
   3 go - ⓔ   4 play - ⓐ
   5 see - ⓓ   6 walk - ⓖ
   7 eat - ⓗ   8 study - ⓕ

Conversation 2

A 2 ⓖ   3 ⓐ   4 ⓔ   5 ⓑ
   6 ⓗ   7 ⓕ   8 ⓒ

B 2 Mr. Kim would like to meet Sumi.
   3 Julie would like to watch that movie.
   4 Chris and Peter want to learn how to drive.
   5 The dog wants to eat that bone.
   6 What would you like to do?
   7 Where do you want to go?
   8 Would you like to stay for dinner?

Conversation 3

C 2 I don't want to watch a movie tonight.
   3 I don't want to take a trip to China this summer.
   4 We don't want to go to the library tomorrow.
   5 We don't want to skip class tonight.
   6 We don't want to cook dinner this evening.

D 1 ⓓ   2 ⓕ   3 ⓑ   4 ⓒ
   5 ⓐ   6 ⓔ

Unit 14 | What's the matter?

Conversation 1

B 1 ⓐ   2 ⓖ   3 ⓔ   4 ⓑ
   5 ⓒ   6 ⓕ   7 ⓗ   8 ⓓ

C 2 I have a sore eye. / My eye hurts.
   3 I have a sore toe. / My toe hurts.
   4 I have a sore wrist. / My wrist hurts.
   5 I have a toothache. / My tooth hurts.
   6 I have a sore elbow. / My elbow hurts.
   7 I have a sore finger. / My finger hurts.
   8 I have a heartache. / My heart hurts.
   9 I have a backache. / My back hurts.
   10 I have a sore arm. / My arm hurts.
   11 I have a earache. / My ear hurts.
   12 I have a sore throat. / My throat hurts.

Conversation 2

B **Health problems**: cut, injury, deafness, drug addiction, allergy, dumb, swollen glands, blindness, fever, the flu, burn, sprain, rash, pain, food poisoning, stroke, nausea, stiffness, itch, runny nose, sore throat
   Diseases: malaria, AIDS, chicken pox, cancer

C 2 sprain   3 cold
   4 food poisoning   5 allergy
   6 burn

Conversation 3

C 2 not worry   3 take
   4 not go   5 listen
   6 see   7 not drink
   8 not eat

Unit 15 | I will take a trip this summer.

Conversation 1

A **Money**: cash, traveler's checks, credit card
   Equipment: sleeping bag, first-aid kit, smartphone, digital camera, video camera
   Baggage: backpack, suitcase, briefcase, fanny pack
   Clothing: bathing suit, shorts, underwear
   Travel Documents: passport, travel insurance, international driver's license, visa, airplane ticket

Conversation 2

B 1 ⓔ   2 ⓓ   3 ⓑ   4 ⓐ
   5 ⓒ

C 2 will be, will take   3 will have
   4 won't win, will make   5 Will, finish

Conversation 3

B 2 is going to travel
   3 is not going to work
   4 are going to graduate
   5 are going to have
   6 is not going to talk
   7 am going to meet
   8 are going to eat

Unit 16 | I want to be a businesswoman.

Conversation 2

B 1 Before we entered the movie theater, we bought tickets. / After we bought tickets, we entered the movie theater.
   2 Before she went to school, she ate breakfast. / After she ate breakfast, she went to school.
   3 Before I watched TV, I finished dinner. / After I finished dinner, I watched TV.
   4 Before he went out with his girlfriend, he did his homework. / After he did his homework, he went out with his girlfriend.
   5 Before they took a test, they studied at the library. / After they studied at the library, they took a test.

C 2 Mary will meet her friends tonight after she finishes class.
   3 Sumi and Jihye are going to watch a movie after their workday is over.
   4 After we take this test, we are going to have a party.
   5 After I get paid, I'm going to buy my girlfriend a nice present.

Conversation 3

C 1 ⓒ   2 ⓕ   3 ⓐ   4 ⓑ
   5 ⓓ   6 ⓔ

D 2 taxi driver   3 engineer
   4 editor   5 enforces the law
   6 designs buildings
   7 sells products/meets clients/goes on business trips
   8 writes computer programs

E 1 false   2 true
   3 true   4 false
   5 false   6 true

F (1) programmer   (2) doctor
   (3) chef   (4) translator

Listen

Unit 01 | It's nice to meet you.

성민 안녕. 난 김성민이야. 네 이름은 뭐니?
줄리 내 이름은 줄리 스미스야. 만나서 반가워. 서… 미안한데, 네 이름이 뭐라고?
성민 내 이름은 김성민이야. 하지만 성민이라고 불러.
줄리 네 이름 철자가 어떻게 되니?
성민 S-U-N-G-M-I-N. 만나서 반가워, 줄리.

줄리 너에 대해 얘기해줄래?
성민 그럼. 난 학생이고 경영학을 전공하고 있어.
줄리 와. 넌 여가시간에 뭐하니?
성민 컴퓨터 게임 하는 걸 좋아해. 너는?
줄리 내 취미는 독서야. 소설을 좋아해.
성민 그거 재미있구나.

성민 한국에 사는 건 어떠니?
줄리 좋아. 난 정말 한국 음식을 좋아해.
성민 네가 가장 좋아하는 음식은 뭐니?
줄리 내가 가장 좋아하는 한국 음식은 불고기야.
성민 맛있지. 내가 가장 좋아하는 미국 음식은 피자야.

Unit 02 | What are you doing now?

릭 안녕, 수미. 바쁘니?
수미 응. 바빠. 오늘 시간 없어.
릭 정말? 지금 뭐 하는데?
수미 나 지금 수학공부 하고 있어.
릭 아, 그럼 오늘 밤 6시 30분에 만날 수 있을까?
수미 미안해. 오늘 밤엔 친구들과 저녁 먹을 거야.

릭 너 존이 어디 있는지 아니?
수미 응. 그는 도서관에 있는데.
릭 도서관이라고! 거기에서 뭐 하는데?
수미 경제학을 공부하고 있어. 내일 중요한 시험이 있거든.
릭 오. 존이 성민이랑 같이 공부하고 있니?
수미 아니, 성민이는 줄리와 함께 있어. 같이 영화 보고 있어.

지혜 너 오늘 아주 즐거워 보인다.
민희 오늘 밤에 콘서트에 갈 거야. 빨리 가고 싶어.
지혜 재미있겠다. 나도 갔으면 좋겠네.
민희 오늘 밤에 뭐 할 건데?
지혜 별로 특별한 건 없어. 하지만 내일은 친구랑 같이 쇼핑하러 갈 예정이야.
민희 돈 너무 많이 쓰지 마.

Unit 03 | Where is it?

여행객 실례합니다. 제가 길을 잃은 것 같네요.
릭 어디를 찾고 계신데요?
여행객 쇼핑센터가 어디에 있습니까?
릭 슈퍼마켓 옆에 있어요.
여행객 잘됐네요. 음… 슈퍼마켓은 어디쯤 있죠?
릭 곧장 가면 있어요. 쉽게 찾을 수 있을 거예요.

존 슈퍼마켓에 어떻게 가야 하나요?
수미 슈퍼마켓이요? 곧장 두 블록을 가세요.
존 네. 그 다음엔 어떻게 하죠?
수미 우회전 하세요. 그 다음 한 블록 직진하세요.
존 알겠습니다.
수미 슈퍼마켓은 왼쪽에 있습니다.
존 길을 알려줘서 고마워요.

줄리 교보문고에 가는 길 좀 알려 줄래?
민희 그래. 우리는 지금 홍대입구역에 있어. 신촌 방향 지하철을 타.
줄리 몇 정거장을 가야 하니?
민희 네 정거장. 그 다음에 충정로역에서 갈아타고 서대문역 방향으로 가.
줄리 알았어.
민희 두 정거장을 가서 광화문역에서 내려. 그리고 2번 출구로 나가면 돼.

Unit 04 | What do you usually do after school?

성민 아침에는 주로 뭐 하니?
릭 보통 7시에 일어나서 옷을 입어.
성민 몇 시에 출근하는데?
릭 9시에 출근해.
성민 매일 일하니?
릭 아니. 토요일과 일요일에는 절대 일 안 해.

민희 너는 항상 저녁을 6시에 먹니?
지혜 응. 너는?
민희 난 보통 6시에 저녁을 먹는데, 가끔은 7시에 먹어.
지혜 저녁 먹고 주로 뭐 하니?
민희 주로 텔레비전을 보거나 책을 읽어.
지혜 나는 아니야. 나는 저녁 먹고 항상 피아노를 쳐.

릭 오늘 저녁에 무슨 계획 있니?
줄리 응. 오늘 저녁에 친구들을 만날 거야.

릭	정말? 친구들을 얼마나 자주 만나니?
줄리	일주일에 두 번 만나. 우리는 종종 여러 가지 많은 일에 대해서 이야기해.
릭	좋은 시간 보내.
줄리	고마워. 그럴게.

Unit 05 | Can you tell me about your family?

줄리	너희 가족에 대해서 말해 줄래?
존	우리 가족은 5명이야. 엄마, 아빠, 남자형제, 여자형제, 그리고 나.
줄리	남자형제는 오빠니 아니면 남동생이니?
존	형이야. 그리고 여자형제는 나보다 어려.
줄리	나는 언니 한 명과 남동생 두 명이 있어.
존	와. 대가족이구나.

성민	아버지는 무슨 일을 하시니?
수미	회사에서 근무하셔. 네 아버지 직업은 뭐니?
성민	아버지는 학교 선생님이고, 어머니는 가정주부야.
수미	네 형과 누나는 뭘 하니?
성민	우리 형은 군대에 있어. 하지만 누나는 대학생이야.
수미	나는 외동딸이야. 나는 형제가 없어.

민희	네 형은 몇 살이니?
릭	우리 형은 25살이야.
민희	음. 우리 언니는 30살이야.
릭	네 부모님은 연세가 어떻게 되시는데?
민희	우리 부모님은 50대 후반이셔.
릭	너는 몇 살이니?
민희	미안해 그건 일급 비밀이야!

Unit 06 | What do you like?

민희	저 애완동물 가게에 들어가 보자. 난 동물들을 아주 좋아해.
성민	그래? 강아지를 좋아하니 고양이를 좋아하니?
민희	강아지. 난 강아지를 아주 좋아해.
성민	어떤 종류의 강아지를 좋아하는데?
민희	요크셔 테리어가 제일 좋아.
성민	그것도 좋지. 하지만 난 리트리버가 더 좋더라.

톰	너 오늘 왜 그렇게 기분이 들떠 있는 거니?
지혜	남자친구와 영화 볼 거야.
톰	재미있겠다. 나 영화 보는 거 좋아해.
지혜	또 내가 좋아하는 식당에도 갈 거야.
톰	어떤 음식을 먹고 싶은데?
지혜	난 이태리 음식을 좋아해. 정말 맛있잖아.

수미	너 괜찮아? 오늘 점심 많이 못 먹었네.

민희	햄버거 안 좋아해. 그래서 하나도 먹지 않았어.
수미	오, 그건 몰랐어.
민희	그래. 그런데 다시 일할 시간이네.
수미	어디 보자… 너 일하기 싫지?
민희	맞아! 내 상사가 정말 싫어.

Unit 07 | What's he like?

성민	나는 데이트 한 번도 못했어.
지나	안됐다. 내가 친구 한 명 소개시켜 줄게.
성민	정말? 어떤 애인데?
지나	아주 괜찮은 애야. 그리고 아주 똑똑해.
성민	그 친구 성격은 좋니?
지나	약간 수줍음을 타는 편인데, 정말 착해.

성민	네 남자친구에 대해서 말해 봐.
지혜	글쎄… 그는 사교적인 사람이야.
성민	어떻게 사교적인데?
지혜	친구를 쉽게 사귀는 편이야. 그리고 항상 농담을 해.
성민	예의도 바른 사람이니?
지혜	응. 항상 나를 위해서 문을 열어 줘.

줄리	너 담배 끊는 게 좋아.
릭	응. 나쁜 습관이니까.
줄리	너는 나쁜 습관들이 많아.
릭	나도 알아. 운동도 더 해야 해.
줄리	그리고 사람들에게 좀더 다정하게 대해.
릭	이봐! 난 모든 게 나쁘지는 않아!

Unit 08 | What does she look like?

릭	새 여자친구가 생겼어.
민희	잘됐다. 어떻게 생겼는데?
릭	아주 예쁘고, 긴 검은 머리를 가졌어.
민희	와. 키는 얼마나 크니?
릭	보통 키야.
민희	언제 한번 만나고 싶다.

줄리	나 운동을 시작해야 할 것 같아.
성민	왜 그렇게 생각하는데?
줄리	나는 과체중이야. 좀더 살을 뺐으면 좋겠어.
성민	내가 보기에는 안 뚱뚱해 보이는데.
줄리	그렇게 말해줘서 고마워.

릭	우리 오늘 밤에도 데이트 할까?
민희	응, 그래.
릭	좋아. 뭐 입을 거야?
민희	난 검은 바지와 흰 블라우스를 입을 거야. 너는?

릭	음… 나는 파란 셔츠와 카키색 바지를 입을 거야.
민희	알았어. 이따 저녁에 보자.

Unit 09 | I can do it.

성민	취미가 있었으면 좋겠어. 나 요즘 심심해.
줄리	수영을 해 봐. 아주 재미있어.
성민	난 수영 못해.
줄리	오… 피아노는 칠 수 있니?
성민	아니. 못 쳐. 난 어떤 악기도 연주할 줄 몰라.
줄리	그럼 뭘 할 수 있는데?

줄리	나 오늘 새 자동차 샀어. 정말 신나.
톰	너 운전할 줄 알아? 그건 몰랐네.
줄리	응. 운전할 수 있어. 근데 잘 하지는 못해.
톰	너 안전 운전자니?
줄리	물론이지. 지금 나랑 타도 돼.
톰	음… 다음에.

지혜	지금 몇 시야?
릭	10시야. 왜?
지혜	진짜? 나 지금 집에 가야 돼.
릭	정말? 그래야 되니?
지혜	응. 가야 해. 아니면 우리 엄마가 무척 화를 낼 거야.
릭	오… 그럼 지금 집에 가는 게 좋겠다.

Unit 10 | What did you do yesterday?

성민	너 오늘 피곤해 보여. 괜찮아?
지혜	밤을 꼴딱 샜어.
성민	왜 그랬어?
지혜	어젯밤에 수학공부 했거든. 오늘 오후에 수학 시험이 있어.
성민	오. 시험 잘 봐.
지혜	고마워.

릭	어제 뭐 했니?
민희	아침에 출근했어.
릭	몇 시에 출근했는데?
민희	아침 9시쯤에. 그리고 7시에 친구를 만났어.
릭	그래. 난 어젯밤에 영화를 봤어.
민희	좋은 시간 보냈기를 바란다.

줄리	좋은 주말 보냈니?
민호	응. 토요일에 영화 봤어.
줄리	정말? 누구랑 함께 갔니?
민호	제일 친한 친구 릭이랑 갔어. 너는?
줄리	난 집에서 하루 종일 TV봤어.

Unit 11 | I had long hair when I was young.

민희	뭘 보고 있니?
지혜	이건 사진첩이야. 옛날 사진들 좀 보고 있어.
민희	얘! 저거 네 사진이니?
지혜	응. 어릴 땐 긴 머리였어.
민희	어릴 때 서울에 살았니?
지혜	아니. 시골에 살았어.

릭	고등학교 시절에 즐겁게 지냈니?
수미	응. 고등학교 때 재미있었어.
릭	정말? 뭐 했었는데?
수미	방과 후에 항상 운동을 했어.
릭	고등학생 때 공부 열심히 했니?
수미	가끔은 하지만 자주 열심히 하진 않았어.

잭	너 중국어 할 수 있니?
민희	예전엔 할 수 있었지만, 더 이상은 아니야.
잭	나도 그래. 난 고등학교 때 배웠어.
민희	학원에 다녔니?
잭	아니, 학원 다닌 적 한 번도 없어.
민희	나는 매일 학원에 다녔어.

Unit 12 | How about going out tonight?

잭	배고파. 나 오늘 점심 먹는 걸 잊어버렸어.
민희	흠… 지금 저녁 먹으러 가자.
잭	좋은 생각이야. 어디로 갈까?
민희	그거 좋은 질문이네.
잭	알았다. 새로 생긴 이탈리안 레스토랑에 가자
민희	그래. 거기서 저녁을 먹는 게 좋겠어.

릭	안녕, 줄리. 어떻게 지내?
줄리	잘 지내.
릭	오늘 밤에 바쁘니?
줄리	아니, 별로. 왜 물어 보는데?
릭	나랑 데이트 하는 거 어때?
줄리	좋아!

지혜	여보세요?
성민	여보세요. 민희랑 통화할 수 있을까요?
지혜	미안하지만, 지금 여기 없는데요.
성민	오, 이런.
지혜	메시지 남기시겠어요?
성민	네. 성민이한테 전화해 달라고 전해 주세요.

Unit 13 | I want to see a movie.

릭 　지루해. 뭐라도 하자.
성민 　좋아. 뭘 하고 싶은데?
릭 　영화 보고 싶어.
성민 　영화는 지루해. 뭔가 다른 걸 하자.
릭 　글쎄… 바에 갈까?
성민 　좋은 생각이야. 가자.

그렉 　저녁 먹을래?
민희 　응. 배고파 죽겠어.
그렉 　어디서 먹고 싶은데?
민희 　난 어디든지 괜찮아.
그렉 　중국식당은 어때?
민희 　좋아. 내가 좋은 장소를 알아. 거기에 가면 되겠다.

수미 　숙제하자.
톰 　싫어. 지금은 숙제하고 싶지 않아.
수미 　음.. 왜 싫은데?
톰 　모르겠어. 그냥 하기 싫어.
수미 　좋아. 그럼 TV보는 건 어때?
톰 　좋은 생각이야. 지금 TV 보고 싶어.

Unit 14 | What's the matter?

지혜 　오, 이런! 너 안색이 안 좋다.
릭 　나 지금 몸이 너무 안 좋아.
지혜 　뭐가 문제야?
릭 　감기 걸렸어.
지혜 　당장 집에 가는 게 좋겠다.
릭 　응. 다시 자야 할 것 같아.

줄리 　지금은 기분이 좀 나아졌니?
릭 　별로. 여전히 아파.
줄리 　증상이 어때?
릭 　콧물이 나고 목이 아파.
줄리 　약 먹었니?
릭 　아니, 아직. 의사한테 곧 갈 거야.

의사 　어디가 아프세요?
릭 　감기에 걸린 것 같아요.
의사 　흠… 좀 봅시다.
릭 　어떻게 해야 하죠?
의사 　아스피린을 좀 먹고, 자면서 휴식을 취하세요.
릭 　고맙습니다. 선생님.

Unit 15 | I will take a trip this summer.

성민 　오늘 왜 그렇게 기분 좋아 보이니?
줄리 　여름방학이 다가오잖아.
성민 　맞아. 이번 여름에 뭐 할 건데?
줄리 　이번 여름에는 여행을 갈 거야.
성민 　멋지다. 어디에 갈 거니?
줄리 　다음 주에 호주에 가.

수미 　오늘 저녁에 뭐 할 거니?
지혜 　남자친구랑 쇼핑하러 갈 거야.
수미 　네 남자친구는 쇼핑하는 거 좋아하니?
지혜 　아니, 싫어해. 하지만 나와 함께 가줄 거야.
수미 　와. 너를 정말로 사랑하나 봐.
지혜 　나도 그렇게 생각해.

릭 　오늘 계획이 뭐야?
줄리 　도서관에 갈 거야.
릭 　왜? 공부할 거니?
줄리 　물론이지. 그리고 나서 성민이랑 저녁 먹을 거야.
릭 　넌 오늘 무지 바쁘겠구나.
줄리 　그러게 말이야.

Unit 16 | I want to be a businesswoman.

민희 　무슨 생각 하고 있니?
성민 　내 미래에 대해서 생각하고 있어.
민희 　정말? 미래에 뭐가 되고 싶은데?
성민 　지금은 잘 모르겠어.
민희 　나는 사업가가 되고 싶어.
성민 　나는 네가 성공할 거라고 믿어.

릭 　이번이 내 마지막 학년이야. 난 내 미래가 걱정돼.
수미 　졸업하고 뭐 할 건데?
릭 　음… 졸업 후에 직장을 구할 거야.
수미 　어디에서 일하고 싶니?
릭 　아직은 잘 모르겠어. 생각해 봐야지.
수미 　난 네가 금방 좋은 일자리를 찾을 거라고 확신해.

지혜 　너 왜 그렇게 웃고 있어? 좋은 소식 있어?
줄리 　아니, 엄청난 소식이 있어. 나 취직했어.
지혜 　잘됐다. 지금 어디서 일하고 있는데?
줄리 　사무실에서 일해. 영업부야.
지혜 　영업? 직무가 뭐니?
줄리 　우리 회사 제품을 판매해야 해. 다른 일도 하고.

How to Pronounce Each Sound

Unit 02

[f]

To make this sound:
1. Touch your lower lip to the tip of your upper teeth.
2. Strongly blow the air out between your lips and teeth. Do not close your lips.
3. This sound is voiceless.

[v]

To make this sound:
1. Touch your lower lip to the tip of your upper teeth.
2. Strongly blow the air out between your lips and teeth. Do not close your lips.
3. This sound is voiced.

Unit 03

[p]

To make this sound:
1. Put your lips together.
2. Breathe out strongly. Make a "popping" sound.
3. This sound is voiceless.

[b]

To make this sound:
1. Put your lips together.
2. Breathe out strongly. Make a "popping" sound.
3. This sound is voiced.

Unit 04

[p]

To make this sound:
1. Stop the flow of air from your mouth by touching your lips together.
2. Breathe out strongly. Make a "popping" sound.
3. This sound is voiceless.

[f]

To make this sound:
1. Touch your lower lip lightly against your upper teeth.
2. Don't use your tongue (rest).
3. This sound is voiced.

Unit 05

[b]

To make this sound:
1. Put your lips together to stop the flow of air.
2. Breathe out strongly. Make a "popping" sound.
3. This sound is voiced.

[v]

To make this sound:
1. Touch your lower lip to the tip of your upper teeth.
2. Don't use your tongue. Push the air out of your mouth.
3. This sound is voiced.

Both [b] and [v] are voiced. But there is one difference. For [b], your lips are together. For [v], your lower lip and upper teeth are together.

Unit 06

[θ]

To make this sound:
1. Put your tongue between your teeth.
2. Push the tip of tongue between your upper and lower teeth.
3. Breathe out.
4. This sound is voiceless.

[ð]

To make this sound:
1. Put your tongue between your teeth.
2. Push the tip of tongue between your upper and

lower teeth.
3. Breathe out.
4. This sound is voiced

[th] can be both voiceless and voiced.

Unit 07

[s]

To make this sound:
1. Place the tip of the tongue very close to the back of your teeth, but not quite touching.
2. Smile like a clown. Then, hiss like a snake.
3. Let the air pass over the top of your tongue. Then, breathe out.
4. This sound is voiceless.

[θ]

To make this sound:
1. Put your tongue between your teeth.
2. Push the tip of tongue between your upper and lower teeth.
3. Breathe out.
4. This sound is voiceless.

Don't confuse this sound with the [s] in sin.
In addition, don't confuse the [θ] sound, like in then, with the [d] in den.

Unit 08

[s]

To make this sound:
1. Place the tip of the tongue very close to the back of your teeth, but not quite touching.
2. Smile like a clown. Then, hiss like a snake.
3. Let the air pass over the top of your tongue. Then, breathe out.
4. This sound is voiceless.

[z]

To make this sound:
1. Touch the sides of your tongue to your tooth ridge.
2. Smile like a clown. Then, hiss like a snake.
3. Let the air pass over the top of your tongue. Then, breathe out.
4. This sound is voiced.

Pronounce [s] and [z] the same way. But there is one difference. [s] is voiceless, but [z] is voiced.

Unit 09

[t]

To make this sound:
1. Touch the tip of your tongue against the ridge behind your upper front teeth.
2. Don't touch your upper teeth to your lower teeth.
3. Quickly move your tongue away from your teeth (tapping). Breathe out.
4. This sound is voiceless.

[d]

To make this sound:
1. Touch the tip of your tongue to the gum ridge behind your upper front teeth.
2. Don't touch your upper teeth to your lower teeth.
3. Quickly move your tongue away from your teeth (tapping). Breathe out.
4. This sound is voiced.

Pronounce [t] and [d] the same way. But there is one difference. [t] is voiceless, but [d] is voiced.

Unit 10

[g]

To make this sound:
1. Press the back of your tongue against the top of your mouth.
2. Quickly move your tongue away.
3. This sound is voiced.

[k]

To make this sound:
1. Press the back of your tongue against the top of your mouth.
2. Quickly move your tongue away.

3 This sound is voiceless.

[g] and [k] are both voiced. But you make the sounds in different ways.

Unit 11

[l]

To make this sound:
1 Touch the tip of your tongue to the bump behind your upper front teeth.
2 Let the air go out your mouth.
3 This sound is voiced.

[r]

To make this sound:
1 Curl the tip of your tongue behind the bump behind your upper front teeth.
2 Move your tongue forward and up. Don't touch the bump behind your upper front teeth.
3 This sound is voiced.

Unit 12

[m]

To make this sound:
1 Press your lips together.
2 Let the air go out your nose. This sound is similar to [p] and [b].
3 Keep your tongue flat.
4 This sound is voiced.

[n]

To make this sound:
1 Touch the tip of your tongue to the bump behind your upper front teeth.
2 Let the air go out your nose.
3 Keep your lips apart.
4 This sound is voiced.

[m] and [n] are both voiced. But you make the sounds in different ways.

Unit 13

[h]

To make this sound:
1 Raise your tongue high in the back of your mouth.
2 Keep your mouth open. Then, push the air out over the back of your tongue.
3 This sound is voiceless.

Don't pronounce the [h] in many words that begin with that letter.

Unit 14

[w]

To make this sound:
1 Raise the back of your tongue high in your mouth.
2 Make your lips round. But don't let them touch. Don't let your lower lip touch your upper teeth.
3 This sound is voiced.

Unit 15

[tʃ]

To make this sound:
1 Put your teeth together. Put your tongue behind your teeth.
2 Shape your lips like a fish's mouth.
3 Quickly move your tongue down and away from your tooth ridge.
4 This sound is voiceless and long.

[ʃ]

To make this sound:
1 Put your teeth together. Put your tongue behind your teeth.
2 Make your lips round. Curve the front of your tongue.
3 Put your tongue on the bump behind your upper front teeth.
4 This sound is voiceless and short.

Unit 16

[dʒ]

To make this sound:
1. Put your teeth close together. Place the tip of your tongue against the ridge behind your upper teeth.
2. Quickly move your tongue down and away from the ridge.
3. Let the air escape against your upper teeth.
4. This sound is voiced.

[tʃ]

To make this sound:
1. Put your teeth close together. Place the tip of your tongue against the ridge behind your upper teeth.
2. Quickly move your tongue down and away from the ridge.
3. Let the air escape against your upper teeth.
4. This sound is voiceless.

Pronounce [dʒ] and [tʃ] the same way. But there is one difference. [dʒ] is voiced, but [tʃ] is voiceless.